Literature
for
Science and
Mathematics

KINDERGARTEN THROUGH GRADE TWELVE

Prepared under the direction of the

Science and Environmental Education Unit
California Department of Education

Publishing Information

Literature for Science and Mathematics, Kindergarten Through Grade Twelve was developed by the Science and Environmental Education Unit, California Department of Education. It was prepared for publication by the staff of the Bureau of Publications. Stephanie Prescott edited the manuscript; Juan Sanchez designed and prepared it for photo-offset production; and Carey Johnson did the typesetting. The document was published by the Department of Education, 721 Capitol Mall, Sacramento, California (mailing address: P.O. Box 944272, Sacramento, CA 94244-2720). It was distributed under the provisions of the Library Distribution Act and *Government Code* Section 11096.

ISBN 0-8011-1066-1

Ordering Information

Copies of this publication are available for $9.50 each, plus sales tax for California residents, from the Bureau of Publications, Sales Unit, California Department of Education, P.O. Box 271, Sacramento, CA 95812-0271; FAX (916) 323-0823.

A list of other publications available from the Department appears on page 136. A complete list may be obtained by writing to the address given above or by calling the Sales Unit at (916) 445-1260.

C O N T E N T S

This publication, *Literature for Science and Mathematics, Kindergarten Through Grade Twelve,* was compiled by a statewide committee composed of science and mathematics teachers, curriculum planners, and librarians employed in schools and in public libraries. Its purpose is to (1) encourage students to read literature related to science and mathematics and to view such reading as a worthwhile activity; (2) help curriculum planners and teachers select books for their science and mathematics courses; and (3) stimulate educators to evaluate and improve their science and mathematics programs.

The committee spent over a year reviewing thousands of books. More than 1,000 titles were selected, representing seven types of literature related to the natural sciences, mathematics, and technology. The selections were then reviewed by more than 100 science educators.

The need for this document was voiced by members of the science and mathematics education communities, including both the *Science Framework* and the *Mathematics Framework* committees. We are pleased to present this publication to you as a companion to these frameworks. As such, it will not only support the curricular principles of the frameworks but will also help educators to implement the instructional techniques suggested in them.

Special acknowledgment is made to Gayland Jordan, Consultant, Science and Environmental Education Unit; Leonard Hull, Consultant (retired), Language Arts and Foreign Languages Unit; and Janet Cole, Education Programs Assistant, Science and Environmental Education Unit. It is because of their untiring efforts and patience that *Literature for Science and Mathematics* has become a reality. We are also grateful to the California educators whose names appear in the Acknowledgments for developing and producing a document that presents such excellent titles in science- and mathematics-related literature.

SALLY MENTOR
Deputy Superintendent
Curriculum and Instructional
Leadership Branch

FRED TEMPES
Associate Superintendent
and Director
Curriculum, Instruction, and
Assessment Division

TOM SACHSE
Manager
Science and Environmental
Education Unit

A
C
K
N
O
W
L
E
D
G
M
E
N
T
S

This annotated bibliography of science- and mathematics-related literature was prepared by a committee composed of educators and librarians, including curriculum planners, science and mathematics teachers of children in kindergarten through grade twelve, and librarians employed in schools and in public libraries. After the list was compiled, it was reviewed by over 100 members of the California science community, including fellows and staff of the California Academy of Science.

The California Department of Education is most grateful for the efforts and contributions of these groups.

Science Literature Committee

Danielle Andrews, Vacaville Unified School District
Stella Baker, Contra Costa County Library
Lauralee Barton, Riverside Unified School District
Carolyn Brook, Scotts Valley Union Elementary School District
Diane Dooley, Holt Union Elementary School District
Joan Felsch, Claremont Unified School District
Linda Huetinck, California State University, Northridge
Joe Huntley, Lakeside Union Elementary School District
Joan T. Janis, University of California, San Diego
Janis Kessler, Bakersfield City Elementary School District
Nancy Koppel, San Jose Unified School District
Barbara Novelli, Pacific Grove Unified School District
Henry M. Pang, Torrance Unified School District
Anne Santer, Kern County Office of Education
Judy Sasges, Santa Clara County Library Administration
Connie Sparks, Los Angeles Unified School District
Jack Swords, Santa Maria–Bonita School District
Nancy Taylor, Ramona Unified School District
Judith Toll, San Leandro Unified School District
Ellis Vance, Fresno County Office of Education
Suzanne Weisker, Vacaville Unified School District
Jeanine Werner, Fresno Unified School District
Jean Wickey, Bakersfield City Elementary School District
Silvia Ybarra, Fresno Unified School District

California Department of Education Staff Members

Gayland Jordan, Consultant, Science and Environmental Education Unit
Leonard Hull, Consultant (retired), Language Arts and Foreign Languages Unit
Janet Cole, Education Programs Assistant, Science and Environmental Education Unit

This publication lists books related to science and mathematics for students in kindergarten through grade twelve. It contains over 1,000 annotated entries on the physical sciences, earth sciences, life sciences, and mathematics. The California Department of Education has published this document to represent the perspectives of educators in both the science and mathematics communities. It is intended to be a companion to the *Science Framework* and to provide science educators with information on superior science-related literature that they can use to implement the concepts of the framework. Similarly, the mathematics books selected are consistent with the principles of the *Mathematics Framework* and are intended to enhance the mathematics curriculum.

Although the natural sciences and mathematics are different disciplines, they have developed together throughout history and depend on each other for ideas and tools. Generally, the word *science* in this document is used to mean the natural sciences. However, the term can also reflect the often-used reference to mathematics as a science.

Purpose

The reading of science-related literature by students can improve their understanding of science concepts, enhance their appreciation of the world of science, and expose them to good literature that addresses philosophical, moral, and ethical values as well as scientific concepts. Similarly, students can enhance their mathematical power through mathematics-related literature and better understand the role of mathematics in their lives.

The purpose of this publication is to serve as a resource for teachers choosing science- and mathematics-related literature for their schools and classrooms. It is a resource that reflects the collective judgment of well-qualified and thoughtful science educators, mathematics educators, school librarians, and public librarians from throughout the state. However, it is intended only as a *guide* to selecting supplementary books for students; the recommended titles are not related to the formal textbook-adoption process and are not meant to be prescriptive in any way.

Selection and Compilation

This document was developed by a committee composed of science and mathematics educators and librarians who have had experience at all grade levels, from kindergarten through grade twelve. The criteria used by the committee to select the entries for the list were (1) the recognized quality of the literature; and (2) the quality of the science or mathematics content, according to the principles set forth in the frameworks. After an entry was nominated by a member of the science literature committee, it was submitted to all members of the committee for verification. The collective judgment of the committee members prevailed in the inclusion or exclusion of any book.

After the committee members made their selections, the titles were submitted to a group of science educators and librarians for their recommendations. In addition, the fellows of the California Academy of Sciences reviewed the books for scientific accuracy. For that review, the books were collected and publicly displayed in the academy's library. Finally, the document was edited, designed, and published by the California Department of Education.

The committee considered the books cited to be especially valuable. Although some titles may be out of print, they may nevertheless be available through public libraries, universities, museums, or specialty bookstores. Materials that are known to be out of print are marked with asterisks (*).

Format and Organization

For ease of use, *Literature for Science and Mathematics* is divided into four sections: Physical Sciences, Earth Sciences, Life Sciences, and Mathematics. Within each section, entries are listed alphabetically by author (by title, for edited volumes). Each entry includes information that will assist educators in choosing and locating supplemental reading for their students. The following example illustrates the format used to present this information.

Type of literature[6]	Grade span[7]	Illustrations[8]
NFI	6–9	I

Aaseng, Nathan.[1] *The Inventors: Nobel Prizes in Chemistry, Physics, and Medicine.*[2] Lerner, 1988.[3]

1001[4] Scientists who won Nobel prizes, their scientific discoveries, and the basic underlying scientific concepts involved in their inventions are presented.[5]

1. Author
2. Title
3. Publisher and date of publication
4. Number used as reference in the subject index
5. Annotation (emphasis on technology, ecology, or folklore noted in brackets)
6. Type of literature, abbreviated as follows:

B	Biography	NFN	Nonfiction narrative
F	Fiction	P	Poetry
NFI	Nonfiction informational	SF	Science fiction

7. Suggested grade span

K–3	Primary	6–9	Middle school
3–6	Elementary	9–12	High school

The grade spans are not prescriptive. They were suggested by members of the science literature committee to give teachers wide latitude in choosing books for their students. The recommended titles may be appropriately used at levels other than those suggested.

8. Characteristic illustrations

I	Illustrations such as paintings, drawings, and charts
P	Photographs
S	Scientific drawings

Further enhancing the usefulness of *Literature for Science and Mathematics* are its five appendixes. Appendix A offers concrete suggestions for incorporating literature into the science curriculum. This appendix also relates the use of literature to the principles of the *Science Framework*.

Appendix B extends the listings in the body of the publication to include selected resources, references, and field guides, which include annotations if the nature of their content is not evident from their titles.

Appendixes C, D, and E contain indexes arranged by subject, author, and title, respectively.

Definitions of Terms

The selection, placement, and annotation of titles for this bibliography are based on the following definitions:

Literature: A body of written work that expresses universal ideas communicated to the reader through its style, clarity, and richness of language. With its layers of complexity, literature both reflects and challenges basic human values. Literature is open to individual interpretation, stimulates emotional involvement, and encourages visualization.

Science- and mathematics-related literature: Literature that incorporates scientific or mathematical subject matter. The literary elements help readers connect their experiences to the concepts presented, enhancing their understanding. Such literature motivates readers to think, seek information, and gain greater knowledge of science and mathematics. Science-related literature should accurately reflect the natural world as we know it. Mathematics-related literature should reflect or illustrate mathematical ideas, tools, and techniques that stimulate the student to think and communicate mathematically.

Physical science: Physics, chemistry, and the related sciences. Physical science is also the base science for earth science and life science. Modern technology and the engineering of machinery, all electrical and electronic devices, and material processing are derived from the principles of physical science.

Earth science: Astronomy, geology, meteorology, and oceanography. Technology based on astronomy has made space exploration possible. Geology has led to the efficient exploration and mining of minerals. Oceanography and meteorology have led to weather forecasting.

Life science: Biology, zoology, botany, physiology, and genetics. Life science is closely related to the other sciences because many life processes can be understood through the principles of physical science. Biotechnology, through such techniques as genetic engineering, is rapidly enabling the development of improved medicines and foods.

Mathematics: The process of searching for patterns and relationships in numbers, shapes, data, and arrangements. Books about computers are included as technology books in this document's mathematics section.

Ecology: A part of natural science, the study of the relationship of living organisms to each other and to their environment. However, in this document, those books carrying an [Ecology] designation extend beyond natural science. Often they advocate changing behavior to conserve resources and reduce pollution. Books so designated would be useful in environmental education studies. Ecology is an important part of environmental education, but the latter also extends into the areas of social science, economics, and politics.

Technology: In this document, generally covers electronics, aviation, computer science, space-craft, chemical processing, transportation, communications, and manufacturing. Technology is closely related to science and can appear to be science. Technology often derives from science and provides tools that enable scientific inquiry. Books with a [Technology] designation often are not concerned with scientific processes.

Science fiction, folklore, and mythology: Science fiction books often explore certain aspects of trends whose implications extend beyond current developments. Books in this category were selected for their literary merit, their scientific or technological accuracy, and their ability to arouse students' interest in science. Books on mythology and folklore are included because they are often explanations of or attempts to organize natural phenomena into meaningful patterns. Both mythology and folklore predate science; all three share the same need to observe and explain the natural world.

The physical sciences are physics and chemistry, the earliest and most basic sciences. The history described in books such as Geraldine Woods's *Science in Ancient Egypt* begins thousands of years ago. Books such as Stephen Hawking's *A Brief History of Time* offer narrative glimpses of the most profound understanding of the real world. The process of science is seen in biographies such as George Gamow's *The Great Physicists from Galileo to Einstein*. At the elementary level, simple informational descriptions of devices and physical processes are offered, such as in *Fire! Fire!* by Gail Gibbons. A few books of poems, such as *Song from Unsung Worlds: Science in Poetry,* edited by Bonnie Bilyeau Gordon, embody the spirit and mystique of science. Books such as Walter Boyne's *Power Behind the Wheel: Creativity and the Evolution of the Automobile* elucidate the principles of the physical sciences and lead to an understanding of the technology of machinery and transportation.

NOTE: Materials that are known to be out of print are marked with asterisks (*).

	Type of literature	Grade span	Illus- trations
Aaseng, Nathan. *The Inventors: Nobel Prizes in Chemistry, Physics, and Medicine.* Lerner, 1988. **1001** Scientists who won Nobel prizes, their scientific discoveries, and the underlying scientific concepts involved in their inventions are presented.	NFI	6–9	I
Abrams, Lawrence F. *Throw It out of Sight! Building and Flying a Hand-Launched Glider.* Dillon Press, 1984. **1002** This book contains illustrated instructions for building a plane that flies.	NFI	6–12	I
Adams, Adrienne. *The Great Valentine's Day Balloon Race.* Macmillan, 1980. **1003** The principles of hot air balloons are introduced in the story of Orson Abbot, a rabbit who builds one for the big race.	NFN	K–3	I
Adkins, Jan. *Moving Heavy Things.* Houghton Mifflin, 1980. **1004** Witty prose and simple line drawings address the problem of moving heavy, unwieldy loads by overcoming friction. Methods discussed include using wedges, levers, jacks, and the block-and-tackle technique.	NFI	3–9	I
Allison, Linda. *The Wild Inside: The Sierra Club's Guide to the Great Outdoors.* Little, Brown, 1988. **1005** This book discusses homes in relation to our environment. It also discusses the electrical and plumbing features of our homes and the variety of creatures with whom we share our homes.	NFI	6–9	I
Alvarez, Luis W. *Alvarez: The Adventures of a Physicist.* Basic Books, 1989. **1006** This autobiography is by a Nobel laureate who helped usher in the atomic age.	B	9–12	P
Apfel, Necia H. *Calendars.* Franklin Watts, 1985. **1007** This book explains the reasons for the development of calendars, the variety of calendars used over the years, and their relationship to the moon's phases and to the seasons.	NFI	6–9	P
Apfel, Necia H. *It's All Relative: Einstein's Theory of Relativity.* Lothrop, Lee and Shepard, 1981. **1008** The basic principles of relativity are introduced. Also included are descriptions of experiments that help explain the concepts of time dilation, black holes, red shift, and the curvature of space.	NFI	9–12	P

	Type of literature	Grade span	Illus- trations
Ardley, Neil. *Music.* Knopf, 1989. **1009** Many musical instruments are shown in photographs; interior views show how desired sounds are created.	NFI	6–9	I
Asch, Frank. *Bear Shadow.* Simon and Schuster, 1988. **1010** This imaginative story will help young children comprehend the rotation of the earth and the movement of shadows.	F	K–3	I
Asimov, Isaac. *Asimov's Chronology of Science and Discovery: How Science Has Shaped the World and How the World Has Affected Science from 4,000,000 B.C. to the Present.* Harper, 1989. **1011** Asimov provides us with an understanding of how science and history are intertwined by pairing scientific discoveries with concurrent world events.	NFN	9–12	P
Asimov, Isaac. *Inside the Atom.* Abelard Schuman, 1974. **1012** Atoms are presented in detail, including their structures, behaviors, and current and future uses.	NFI	6–12	I
Asimov, Isaac. *I, Robot.* Doubleday, 1963. **1013** These science fiction stories about "positronic" robots explain why the famous three laws of robotics were developed. [Technology]	SF	9–12	
Atkins, Peter W. *Molecules.* Freeman, 1987. **1014** The abstract concept of molecules is related to everyday experiences. The illustrations help to clarify the explanations.	NFN	9–12	I
Aylesworth, Thomas G. *The Alchemists: Magic into Science.* Addison-Wesley, 1973. **1015** This entertaining journey through the history of alchemy covers its relationship to modern science.	NFN	6–9	I
Barton, Byron. *Machines at Work.* Crowell, 1987. **1016** A simple picture book introduces workers and heavy equipment at a construction site. The heavy lines used for the illustrations make the large machines look powerful. [Technology]	F	K–3	I
Baum, Arline, and Joseph Baum. *Opt: An Illusionary Tale.* Viking, 1987. **1017** A reader cannot resist solving these puzzles and illusions. Fortunately, the last chapter explains them.	NFN	3–6	I
Benford, Gregory. *Time-Scape.* Simon and Schuster, 1980. **1018** In this science fiction tale, scientists of the future try sending a message to the past. This book depicts scientists at work.	SF	9–12	
Berger, Melvin. *Atoms, Molecules, and Quarks.* Putnam, 1986. **1019** A beginning chemistry book that includes history, experiments, and an excellent explanation of the "particle zoo" that makes up matter.	NFI	9–12	I
Berger, Melvin. *The Science of Music.* Harper, 1989. **1020** This academic look at the physics of musical sounds defines sound, gives a brief history for each group of instruments, discusses their specific acoustical merits, describes the processes involved in making a recording, and explains the variety of playback equipment available today.	NFI	6–9	P

	Type of literature	Grade span	Illus-trations
Beshore, George. *Science in Ancient China.* Franklin Watts, 1988. **1021** The many practical inventions developed by the Chinese are introduced in this book, which also discusses how these inventions improved the quality of daily life in China. Recent discoveries made by Western physicists that concur with ancient Chinese scholars' theories are also discussed.	NFI	6–9	I
Beshore, George. *Science in Early Islamic Culture.* Franklin Watts, 1988. **1022** Early Middle Eastern scholars and their many contributions to world-wide knowledge are discussed. This book emphasizes the base these scholars provided for modern scientific methods.	NFI	6–9	I
Billings, Charlene. *Fiber Optics: Bright New Way to Communicate.* Putnam, 1986. **1023** Defining the technology of optical fibers as a method of transmitting information through light, this book describes the many uses of optical fibers in such diverse fields as medicine, shopping, conferences, entertainment, and basic communication. [Technology]	NFN	9–12	P
Billings, Charlene. *Superconductivity: From Discovery to Breakthrough.* Dutton, 1991. **1024** This book introduces the history, theories, structure, and construction of superconductors. [Technology]	NFI	9–12	P
Blohm, Hans, Stafford Beer, and David Suzuki. *Pebbles to Computers: The Thread.* Oxford, 1987. **1025** This history of the computer starts with the computations of early civilizations and continues through the people and the inventions that were important in the process leading to the invention of the computer. [Technology].	NFN	6–12	P
Boyne, Walter J. *Power Behind the Wheel: Creativity and the Evolution of the Automobile.* Abbeville, 1991. **1026** The technology and design of automobiles are the focus of this in-depth account. It includes a projection into the future and excellent photographs of classic cars. [Technology]	NFN	6–12	P
Boyne, Walter J. *The Smithsonian Book of Flight for Young People.* Macmillan, 1988. **1027** This history of American flight includes the effects of research and wars on the airplane industry. The color photographs in this book are marvelous. [Technology]	NFI	6–12	P
Brand, Stewart. *The Media Lab: Inventing the Future at MIT.* Viking, 1987. **1028** In this inside report on the research at MIT's communications laboratory, the author stirs the imagination with the possible applications of computers. [Technology]	NFN	9–12	
Branley, Franklyn M. *Gravity Is a Mystery.* Harper, 1986. **1029** Gravity is clearly explained, as is the relationship between weight and gravity.	NFI	3–6	I

	Type of literature	Grade span	Illustrations
Brenner, Martha. *Fireworks Tonight!* Hastings House, 1986. **1030** This is a definitive book on fireworks. It includes the history of fireworks, methods of producing them, and the varieties currently available, as well as regulations and safety guidelines. [Technology]	NFI	6–12	P
Bronowski, Jacob. *The Ascent of Man.* Little, Brown, 1976. **1031** In this history of science, Bronowski explores the connections among many of the scientific achievements of our civilization.	NFN	9–12	P
Brown, A. E., and H. A. Jeffott, Jr. *Absolutely Mad Inventions.* Dover, 1970. **1032** The authors present inventions, just as the inventors submitted them to the United States Patent Office. [Technology]	NFI	6–12	I
Brown, Ruth. *If at First You Do Not See.* Holt, Rinehart and Winston, 1983. **1033** In this story an adventuresome caterpillar discovers many scary monsters that readers recognize as clever optical illusions.	F	K–3	I
Burgess, Jeremy. *Microcosmos.* Cambridge, 1987. **1034** These beautiful photographs taken through an electron microscope introduce a fascinating world we normally cannot see.	NFI	6–12	P
Burke, James. *The Day the Universe Changed.* Little, Brown, 1987. **1035** Eight extraordinary discoveries that changed humans' perception of knowledge and the world are described eloquently. The pictures, illustrations, and drawings are historical source materials. [Technology]	NFN	9–12	I
Burkig, Valerie. *Photonics: The New Science of Light.* Enslow, 1986. **1036** The author explains light, lasers, and mirrors before describing fiber optics and holography and their uses in high technology. [Technology]	NFN	6–9	P
Burn, Doris. *Andrew Henry's Meadow.* Coward-McCann, 1965. **1037** When a boy's intricate inventions become disruptive, his family encourages him to move into a nearby meadow. Henry spends the summer constructing marvelous inventions. [Ecology]	F	K–6	I
Burns, Marilyn. *The Book of Think: Or How to Solve Problems Twice Your Size.* Little, Brown, 1976. **1038** This book on problem solving and critical thinking presents a series of mental exercises leading to the realization that there is more than one way to solve a problem.	NFI	9–12	I
Burns, Marilyn. *This Book Is About Time.* Little, Brown, 1978. **1039** The history of time is explored. Also included are many amusing facts, a discussion of biological clocks, and activities for making timepieces.	NFI	3–9	I
Bushey, Jerry. *Monster Trucks and Other Giant Machines on Wheels.* Carolrhoda, 1985. **1040** Twelve giant machines are introduced with color photographs and facts about their sizes, uses, and costs. [Technology]	F	K–3	P
Calhoun, Mary. *Hot-Air Henry.* William Morrow, 1984. **1041** The activity of hot air ballooning is introduced through Henry, who accidentally takes off on a solo flight, finally lands, and returns home.	F	K–3	I

PHYSICAL SCIENCES   **5**

	Type of literature	Grade span	Illustrations
Card, Orson Scott. *Ender's Game.* Tor, 1985. **1042** In this science fiction tale, the planet Earth's military commander faces aliens he has defeated twice, but he worries about defeating them a third time.	SF	9–12	
Carson, Rachel. *Silent Spring.* Houghton Mifflin, 1987. **1043** This classic book was one of the first addressing the dangers of the indiscriminate use of pesticides. [Ecology]	NFN	9–12	
Caselli, Giovanni. *The Roman Empire and the Dark Ages.* THE HISTORY OF EVERYDAY THINGS series. Bedrick, 1985. **1044** The developments of Roman machines, weapons, and household objects are logically and chronologically explained in this beautifully illustrated book. [Technology]	NFI	6–12	I
Chadwick, Roxane. *Anne Morrow Lindbergh: Pilot and Poet.* Lerner, 1987. **1045** This biography emphasizes Anne's love of family, exploration, writing, and conservation. [Technology]	B	3–6	P
Chaisson, Eric. *Relatively Speaking: Relativity, Black Holes, and the Fate of the Universe.* Norton, 1990. **1046** The author discusses the questions raised by the observed motion of the galaxies and explores the theories of relativity, time dilation, and curved space.	NFI	9–12	I
Charles, Oz. *How Is a Crayon Made?* Simon and Schuster, 1990. **1047** Bright colors illustrate the processes involved in making crayons. [Technology]	NFI	K–6	P
Cheney, Margaret. *Tesla, Man out of Time.* Dell, 1983. **1048** This biography looks at Nikola Tesla's major scientific contributions as well as his personal life.	B	9–12	
Cobb, Vicki. *Why Doesn't the Earth Fall Up? And Other Not Such Dumb Questions About Motion.* Dutton, 1989. **1049** Force, motion, and gravity are explained in this book. The illustrations are cartoon drawings that enhance an understanding of each concept. The author introduces early scientists and discusses the logic and reasoning behind their concepts and theories.	NFN	3–6	I
Corrick, James. *Recent Revolutions in Chemistry.* Franklin Watts, 1986. **1050** The author makes a powerful statement about the impact of chemistry and its relationship to other disciplines. He concludes that a knowledge of chemistry is essential to understanding the issues facing the modern world.	NFI	6–12	P
Cottrell, William H., Jr. *The Book of Fire.* Mountain Press, 1989. **1051** Using simple words and vivid diagrams, the author explains the complex science of fire.	NFI	9–12	I
Curie, Eve. *Madame Curie.* Da Capo, 1986. **1052** This classic biography, written by Marie Curie's daughter, includes personal and historical information about the family as well as information about Madame Curie's scientific accomplishments.	B	9–12	

	Type of literature	Grade span	Illustrations
De Camp, L. Sprague. *The Ancient Engineers.* Ballantine, 1987. **1053** This historical account stresses the importance of engineers and their efforts to use the material world around them to create an easier, more comfortable life. [Technology]	NFI	9–12	I
De Paola, Tomie. *The Popcorn Book.* Holiday House, 1978. **1054** As twins make a batch of popcorn, they learn about its history, cultivation, and cooking methods.	NFN	K–3	I
Dickinson, Peter. *The Weathermonger.* Dell, 1988. **1055** In this science fiction tale Jeff and Sally search England to find the disorder that is causing people to fear machines.	SF	6–9	
Dorros, Arthur. *Me and My Shadow.* Scholastic, 1990. **1056** The author provides easy investigations of principles governing shadows and then extends these principles to X-rays and sonograms.	F	K–3	I
Einstein, Albert. *Ideas and Opinions.* Crown Publishers, 1985. **1057** Einstein himself supervised the gathering of this collection of his popular writings.	NFN	9–12	
Einstein, Albert. *Relativity: The Special and General Theory.* Crown Publishers, 1961. **1058** Einstein explains his theories so clearly and effectively that advanced science students should benefit greatly from reading his own words.	NFI	9–12	
Epstein, Samuel, and Beryl Epstein. *Tunnels.* Little, Brown, 1985. **1059** This is a comprehensive overview of tunnels found throughout the world, with many drawings and photographs.	NFI	6–12	P
Faraday, Michael. *The Chemical History of a Candle.* Cherokee Books, 1978. **1060** This is Faraday's famous Christmas Lecture for the Royal Institution of London. Some consider it perhaps to be the greatest example of scientific thinking ever addressed specifically to young people.	NFN	9–12	
Feldbaum, Carl, and Ronald J. Bee. *Looking the Tiger in the Eye: Confronting the Nuclear Threat.* Harper, 1988. **1061** This book focuses on the history of the social and political climates that surrounded the development and use of nuclear weapons and discusses society's responsibility for future decisions.	NFN	6–12	
Ferguson, Kitty. *Black Holes in Space-Time.* Franklin Watts, 1991. **1062** Current, accepted information concerning black holes and related phenomena are described in this book that also includes the opposing theories.	NFI	9–12	P
Feynman, Richard. *QED: The Strange Theory of Light and Matter.* Princeton, 1985. **1063** A leading theoretical physicist presents the essentials of quantum electrodynamics, facilitating an understanding of quarks and related topics in high-energy physics.	NFI	9–12	

	Type of literature	Grade span	Illus- trations
Feynman, Richard. *Surely You're Joking, Mr. Feynman! Adventures of a Curious Character.* Bantam, 1989. **1064** These humorous short stories show how a great physicist's scientific mind perceives the world around him.	B	9–12	
Filson, Brent. *Exploring with Lasers.* Julian Messner, 1984. **1065** The author describes the historical and scientific backgrounds and stresses the important roles they play in medicine, industry, art, entertainment, and the military. [Technology]	NFN	3–9	I
Flanagan, Dennis. *Flanagan's Version: A Spectator's Guide to Science on the Eve of the Twenty-First Century.* Random House, 1989. **1066** These seven essays by the former editor of *Scientific American* include numerous examples to readers in distinguishing between pseudo and real science.	NFN	9–12	
Fleisher, Paul. *Secrets of the Universe: Discovering the Universal Laws of Science.* Macmillan, 1987. **1067** The author explains the laws of physics in a logical manner, with both illustrations and experiments to clarify these concepts.	NFI	6–12	I
Foley, Gerald, and Charlotte Nassim. *The Energy Question.* Viking, 1988. **1068** In this book the authors discuss sources of energy, explain how energy is absorbed and reflected by the earth, and suggest wise choices in the use of energy. [Ecology]	NFN	9–12	
Forward, Robert L. *Dragon's Egg.* Ballantine, 1983. **1069** In this science fiction novel, the human observers interact with a race that evolved on the surface of a neutron star and live within a highly compressed time scale. This tale provides an accurate portrayal of scientists at work.	SF	9–12	
Freedman, Russell. *The Wright Brothers: How They Invented the Airplane.* Holiday House, 1991. **1070** Original pictures and primary sources add spice to this biography that highlights the research, experiments, and testing necessary for these first powered, sustained, and controlled airplane flights. [Technology]	B	6–12	P
Freeman, Don. *A Rainbow of My Own.* Puffin, 1978. **1071** In this simple story a little boy wishes for a rainbow. When the sun shines through a fish bowl, a rainbow appears for him.	F	K–3	I
Fritz, Jean. *What's the Big Idea, Ben Franklin?* Putnam, 1982. **1072** This biography stresses Ben Franklin's creative thinking, hard work, desire to learn, and testing of his knowledge. His creative ideas and skills that made life easier and richer for his family, neighbors, and the new country are discussed.	B	3–6	I
Fritz, Jean. *Who's That Stepping on Plymouth Rock?* Putnam, 1975. **1073** This is a simple history story that recounts what has happened to this rock since the Pilgrims from the Mayflower first stepped on it.	NFN	3–6	I

	Type of literature	Grade span	Illustrations
Gallant, Roy A. *Explorers of the Atom.* Doubleday, 1974. **1074** This discussion of atoms includes diagrams and photographs that illustrate the historical quest to understand their structures, the application of the knowledge of radioisotopes, the uses of atomic energy, and the pollution problems radioactivity poses.	B	9–12	P
Gamow, George. *The Great Physicists from Galileo to Einstein.* Dover, 1988. **1075** In this book eight great scientific figures and their theories are highlighted, giving readers a historical overview.	B	9–12	
Gamow, George. *Mr. Thompkins in Paperback.* Cambridge, 1967. **1076** In this book, Mr. Thompkins, a bank clerk, attends lectures on modern physics and always falls asleep. Through his dreams readers experience the strange worlds of subatomic particles, a rapidly expanding universe, and a town with a low speed of light.	NFN	9–12	I
Gardner, Martin. *The New Ambidextrous Universe: Symmetry and Asymmetry from Mirror Reflections to Superstrings.* W. H. Freeman, 1991. **1077** This book is a treasure house of complex, thought-provoking ideas that are introduced in a clear and entertaining manner.	NFI	9–12	
Gardner, Martin E. *The Sacred Beetle and Other Great Essays in Science.* Prometheus, 1984. **1078** Thirty-two thought-provoking essays by noted scholars and scientists address a variety of scientific concepts.	NFN	9–12	
Gardner, Robert. *Science and Sports.* VENTURE series. Edited by Henry Rasot. Franklin Watts, 1988. **1079** The applications of physical principles are introduced and explained in a practical form as they apply to athletes.	NFI	6–9	
Gay, Kathlyn. *Silent Killers: Radon and Other Hazards.* IMPACT series. Edited by M. Kline. Franklin Watts, 1988. **1080** Dangerous chemicals, gases, and metals are described in this book that also suggests steps individuals can take to protect themselves and the environment against these hazards. [Ecology]	NFI	6–12	P
Gelman, Rita Golden. *What Are Scientists? What Do They Do?* Scholastic, 1991. **1081** After reading this book, children will understand that scientists are very curious people who try to find answers to questions.	NFN	K–3	I
Gibbons, Gail. *Fire! Fire!* Harper, 1987. **1082** The author describes the steps the fire department takes to put out fires in four different locations: a city apartment, a country barn, a forest, and a pier on the waterfront.	NFI	K–3	I
Gibbons, Tony. *Submarines.* Lerner, 1987. **1083** A definitive look at submarines, this book covers how they work, how they function, and what future uses they might have.	NFI	K–6	I

	Type of literature	Grade span	Illustrations
Gibson, William. *Neuromancer.* Ace, 1984. **1084** This science fiction tale portrays a world dominated by microelectronic technology. The main character is assigned dangerous missions as he roams the world's computer network.	SF	9–12	
Gilmore, C. P. *The Scanning Electron Microscope: World of the Infinitely Small.* New York Geographic Society, n.d. **1085** The electron micrograph introduces us to a world we cannot see with the naked eye. The pictures shown in this book vary from insects' eyes to body cells to the effects of DDT on birds' eggs. [Technology]	NFI	3–9	P
Goudsmit, Samuel, and others. *Time.* Time-Life, 1966. **1086** All facets of time are explored in a manner that transcends the disciplines of science.	NFI	9–12	P
Greene, Herb. *Building to Last: Architecture as Ongoing Art.* Architectural Book Publishing, 1981. **1087** The author discusses architects' wishes to build structures that will last, beautify a city, and respond to the needs of both present and future generations.	NFI	9–12	I
Grey, Vivian. *The Chemist Who Lost His Head: The Story of Antoine Lavoisier.* Putnam, 1982. **1088** This biography concentrates on the scientific career of Antoine Laurent Lavoisier, who was executed on May 8, 1784. He was the man most responsible for developing chemistry into an exact science with his insistence on accurate measurements in experiments.	B	6–12	I
Grillone, Lisa, and Joseph Gennaro. *Small Worlds Close Up.* Crown Publishers, 1987. **1089** A scanning electron microscope was used to take these close-up black-and-white photographs of ordinary objects. They reveal intriguing details and unexpected structures.	NFI	3–9	P
Haines, Gail Kay. *Test-Tube Mysteries.* Dodd, Mead, 1982. **1090** These short stories present puzzling scientific mysteries with surprising answers. See also the author's *Micro Mysteries: Stories of Scientific Detection.* (Putnam, 1990).	NFI	9–12	
Haldeman, Joe. *The Forever War.* Avon, 1991. **1091** In this science fiction tale, Private William Mandella is drafted into a war that he does not want to fight. As the story develops, he has to deal with his feelings about the war and the time distortions caused by faster-than-flight travel.	SF	9–12	
Harris, Jacqueline L. *Science in Ancient Rome.* Franklin Watts, 1988. **1092** This book chronicles the Roman practice of applying other civilizations' scientific knowledge to improve the quality of Romans' lives.	NFI	6–9	I
Hart, Ivor B. *The Great Physicists.* Ayer, 1927. **1093** Many physicists are introduced in this book, from the ancient physicists Pythagoras and Archimedes to Galileo, Pascal, Boyle, and, finally, Newton and Joule.	B	9–12	I

	Type of literature	Grade span	Illustrations

Hawkes, Nigel. *Nuclear Power.* Rourke, 1990.

   1094 The author presents general information about atomic power and its uses. [Technology]

| NFI | 6–12 | I |

Hawking, Stephen W. *A Brief History of Time: From the Big Bang to Black Holes.* Bantam, 1990.

   1095 This unique physicist and cosmologist holds the reader captive as he elucidates complex theory and philosophy for a lay audience.

| NFN | 9–12 | |

Hazen, Robert M. *The Breakthrough: The Race for the Superconductor.* Ballantine, 1989.

   1096 This story describes the research that led to the development of a practical superconductor.

| NFN | 9–12 | |

Hoban, Tana. *Look! Look! Look!* Greenwillow, 1988.

   1097 This book contains photographs that inspire a second look at everyday artifacts and encourage the development of observational skills.

| NFI | K–3 | P |

Hopkins, Lee Bennett. *Click, Rumble, Roar: Poems About Machines*. Crowell, 1987.

   1098 This book of poetry is about machines and the different sounds they make.

| P | 3–9 | I |

Howard, Fred. *Wilbur and Orville: A Biography of the Wright Brothers.* Ballantine, 1988.

   1099 A devotee of aviation will enjoy this very detailed biography of the Wright brothers. [Technology]

| B | 9–12 | P |

Isaacson, Philip. *Round Buildings, Square Buildings, and Buildings That Wiggle like a Fish.* Knopf, 1990.

   1100 The absorbing color photographs of these buildings show the blending of art, architecture, and engineering and illustrate the power of architecture's influence. [Technology]

| NFI | 3–9 | P |

Jaffe, Bernard. *Crucibles: The Story of Chemistry from Ancient Alchemy to Nuclear Fission.* Dover, 1976.

   1101 This book describes and personalizes the lives of the great chemists and discusses their discoveries.

| NFN | 9–12 | |

Jespersen, James, and Jane Fitz-Randolph. *From Quarks to Quasars: A Tour of the Universe.* Macmillan, 1987.

   1102 This book provides a perspective of our universe as it describes how cosmologists, astronomers, and physicists, using observation and measurement, overcame superstitions and mythology in the search for facts.

| NFI | 9–12 | I |

Jonas, Ann. *Color Dance.* Greenwillow, 1989.

   1103 The nature of primary and secondary colors is explained in this creative book, which also shows the effects of white, gray, and black on the other colors.

| NFI | K–3 | I |

Kaufman, William J. *Relativity and Cosmology.* Harper, 1979.

   1104 Modern topics on astronomy, such as relativity, black holes, quasars, and the fate of the universe, are woven together in this book.

| NFI | 9–12 | |

	Type of literature	Grade span	Illus-trations
Kolb, Kenneth E., and Doris Kolb. *Glass: Its Many Facets.* Enslow, 1988. **1105** This book describes glass through its history, its different forms, and its manufacturing processes, and identifies glass made for specific uses, such as sports equipment, lenses, buildings, and science.	NFI	6–9	I
Kumin, Maxine. *The Microscope.* Harper, 1984. **1106** Written in rhyme, this amusing book chronicles the story of Anton von Leuwenhoek, the father of microscopy.	NFI	3–6	I
Lampton, Christopher. *Bathtubs, Slides, Roller Coaster Rails: Simple Machines That Are Really Inclined Planes.* Millbrook, 1991. **1107** Charming illustrations accompany explanations about the inclined planes, in theory and practice, and the problems with friction they overcome.	NFI	K–6	I
Lampton, Christopher. *Marbles, Roller Skates, Doorknobs: Simple Machines That Are Really Wheels.* Millbrook, 1991. **1108** Clever illustrations in this book accompany explanations of the wheel in its many varieties. Also discussed is the wheel's relationship to balls and gears, problems caused by friction, and the working together of wheels to form simple and complex machines.	NFI	K–6	I
Lampton, Christopher. *Seesaws, Nutcrackers, Brooms: Simple Machines That Are Really Levers.* Millbrook, 1991. **1109** The delightful illustrations in this book accompany explanations for levers, tasks they help accomplish, the use of levers to gain a mechanical advantage, and levers commonly used.	NFI	K–6	I
Lampton, Christopher. *Thomas Alva Edison.* Franklin Watts, 1988. **1110** This biography chronicles the American inventor's life and work.	B	6–9	
Larsen, Rebecca. *Oppenheimer and the Atomic Bomb.* Franklin Watts, 1988. **1111** This biography of Oppenheimer, the brilliant physicist who played a key role in the atomic bomb's development, focuses on the years during and just after the development of the atomic bomb. The awards and acknowledgments Oppenheimer received late in life are also discussed. [Technology]	NFN	9–12	P
LeGuin, Ursula. *The Dispossessed: An Ambiguous Utopia.* Avon, 1976. **1112** In this science fiction tale, one of the galaxy's greatest physicists visits the mother planet, Urras, to learn and share. His visit causes conflict, and each society then must reexamine its values.	SF	9–12	
Leicester, Henry. *Historical Background of Chemistry.* Dover, 1971. **1113** In this history of chemistry that goes up to mid-1950s, Leicester traces the interrelationships of chemical concepts and devotes his attention to earlier periods when chemistry was not recognized as a science in its own right. This book is suitable for advanced readers.	NFI	9–12	P
L'Engle, Madeleine. *A Wrinkle in Time.* Ballantine, 1984. **1114** In this science fiction fantasy, the children search for their scientist father through time and space. After many exciting adventures, they finally save him, and everyone returns home to a loving family.	F	6–9	

	Type of literature	Grade span	Illus-trations
Levi, Primo. *The Periodic Table.* Schocken, 1986. **1115** Each essay in this book is named after an element in the periodic table. Most essays detail an experience the author has had with that element. This highly readable book is an absolute must for chemistry students.	B	9–12	
Ley, Willy. *The Discovery of the Elements.* Delacorte, 1968. **1116** This story of the discovery of 104 chemical elements from the nine elements known to ancient man is woven from historical vignettes. The narrative provides insight into the scientific process as well as modern scientific understanding.	NFN	9–12	I
Lindbergh, Charles A. *The Spirit of St. Louis.* Macmillan, 1975. **1117** This is Lindbergh's account of both his preparations for his flight from New York to Paris and the flight itself. [Technology]	B	9–12	
Livingston, Dorothy A. Michelson. *Master of Light: A Biography of Albert Michelson.* Scribner's, 1973. **1118** Albert Michelson's daughter wrote this biography about her father and their family. She includes information about his work measuring the speed of light and his contributions to the theory of relativity.	B	9–12	I
Macaulay, David. *Cathedral.* Houghton Mifflin, 1981. **1119** Detailed black-and-white line drawings enliven descriptions of the years of work involved in the construction of a Gothic French cathedral. This book would be an interesting accompaniment to the study of simple machines, basic engineering, or construction techniques.	NFN	6–9	I
Macaulay, David. *The Way Things Work.* Houghton Mifflin, 1988. **1120** In this introduction to technology, machines are grouped by the principles governing their actions. [Technology]	NFI	3–12	I
Maccarone, Grace, Nancy Krullk, and Jolie Epstein. *Real Robots.* Scholastic, 1985. **1121** Robots currently in use are defined and classified. Color photographs show the variety of working robots available. [Technology]	NFI	K–6	P
McGowen, Tom. *Chemistry: The Birth of a Science.* Franklin Watts, 1989. **1122** Chemistry's fascinating history is covered in this book, which starts with early alchemy and continues until chemistry becomes a legitimate scientific discipline. The book is nontechnical enough for young scientists who do not have a formal background in chemistry.	NFN	9–12	I
McGrath, Susan. *Fun with Physics.* National Geographic Society, 1986. **1123** Spectacular photographs enhance the explanations of the involvement of physics in all aspects of life—from sports to nature to homes.	NFI	6–12	P
McKie, Robin. *Lasers.* Franklin Watts, 1983. **1124** Laser technology is covered, laser parts are shown, and their specialized uses are presented. [Technology]	NFI	6–12	I
McKie, Robin. *Science Frontiers: Energy.* Hampstead, 1989. **1125** Energy science is defined, and the sources of energy are explored and explained. The many diagrams and photographs enhance descriptions of the research and technology involved in locating energy sources and developing potential sources of power for worldwide use.	NFI	K–6	I

	Type of literature	Grade span	Illus-trations
Math, Irwin. *Wires and Watts: Understanding and Using Electricity.* Macmillan, 1988. **1126** Electricity and magnetism are explained. The hands-on projects described are designed to produce working models.	NFI	6–12	I
Mayers, Florence Cassen. *The ABC National Air and Space Museum.* Harry Abrams, 1979. **1127** Color aviation photographs from early aviation to space-age technology introduce each alphabet letter. The narrations that accompany each photograph are sophisticated. [Technology]	NFI	3–12	P
Milne, Lorus J., and Margery Milne. *Nature's Great Carbon Cycle.* Atheneum, 1983. **1128** Carbon and the importance of the carbon cycle are addressed in this book. The author also looks at the development of atmospheric carbon, decomposition, and fossil fuels. [Ecology]	NFI	9–12	I
Mitgutsch, Ali. *From Milk to Ice Cream.* Carolrhoda, 1981. **1129** Brief descriptions of the processes involved in manufacturing ice cream are enhanced with colorful illustrations. [Technology]	NFI	K–3	I
Moeri, Louise. *Downwind.* Dell, 1987. **1130** This science fiction thriller describes an accident at a nuclear power plant that creates panic in the population. [Technology]	F	3–9	
Morrison, Philip, Phylis Morrison, and the office of Charles and Ray Eames. *Powers of Ten.* Scientific American, 1982. **1131** This book describes a journey through a difference in magnitude of 42 powers of ten. Beautiful photographs illustrate the journey from the largest dimension of the universe to the dimension of protons and quarks.	NFI	6–12	P
Mott, Lawrie, and Karey Snyder. *Pesticide Alert: A Guide to Pesticides in Fruits and Vegetables.* Sierra Club Books, 1988. **1132** The authors argue that we must strike a balance between the use of pesticides and losses of food products. They also recommend methods for both removing pesticides from foods and for preventing the destruction of crops. [Ecology]	NFN	9–12	P
Myers, Norman. *Gaia: An Atlas of Planet Management.* Doubleday, 1984. **1133** Available environmental data, maps, and charts are organized and analyzed. The authors propose that we find an opportunity to redirect our energies toward planetwide efforts to wisely manage our resources. [Ecology]	NFR	9–12	P
National Geographic Society Staff. *Small Inventions That Make a Big Difference: Book for World Explorers.* National Geographic Society, 1984. **1134** This collection includes biographies of inventors, descriptions of their inventions, and the benefits we derive from the inventions. Photographs and drawings enhance the text.	NFI	9–12	I
Newton at the Bat: The Science in Sports. Edited by Eric Schrier and William Allman. Macmillan, 1987. **1135** In these essays experts look at the physics, physiology, aerodynamics, and technology involved in a wide range of popular sports.	NFI	9–12	

	Type of literature	Grade span	Illustrations
On the Shoulders of Giants: New Approaches to Numeracy. Edited by Lynn Arthur Steen. National Academy, 1990. **1136** The author uses the strands of dimension, quantity, uncertainty, change, and shape to explore fundamental changes in the science of mathematics, which has been transformed by computers, new concepts, and new methods.	NFN	9–12	
Pagels, Heinz. ***The Cosmic Code: Quantum Physics as the Language of Nature.*** Bantam, 1984. **1137** The author introduces physics, quantum mechanics, the role of probability in quantum mechanics, matter, atoms, molecules, vacuums, and gauge field theories.	NFN	9–12	
A Passion to Know: 20 Profiles in Science. Edited by Allen L. Hammond. Scribner's, 1984. **1138** This collection of short biographies introduces scientists from a variety of scientific fields.	NFN	9–12	
Pelta, Kathy. ***Bridging the Golden Gate.*** Lerner, 1987. **1139** The author describes the building of the Golden Gate Bridge and points out the skills in science, mathematics, design, and construction needed to complete this project. [Technology]	NFI	3–9	P
Penrose, Roger. ***The Emperor's New Mind: Concerning Computers, Minds, and the Laws of Physics.*** Oxford, 1989. **1140** An eminent physicist explains that there are facets of thinking that can never be emulated by machines. He then examines what physics and mathematics can tell us about the human mind.	NFN	9–12	
The Physical World. Edited by Martin Sherwood and Christine Sutton. Oxford, 1988. **1141** Photographs, drawings, and sidebars with interesting facts and notes make this book a fascinating exploration of physics, chemistry, weather, and astronomy.	NFI	3–9	I
Pringle, Laurence. ***Nuclear Energy: Troubled Past, Uncertain Future.*** Macmillan, 1989. **1142** This book presents an overview of nuclear power's history and development. The author uses information and examples obtained worldwide as he presents the views of both proponents and opponents of nuclear power. [Technology]	NFI	6–9	I
Regis, Ed. ***Great Mambo Chicken and the Transhuman Condition.*** Addison-Wesley, 1991. **1143** The author looks at future technology, introducing scientists who are working on projects slightly beyond conventional research yet whose theories might change history.	NFN	9–12	
Regis, Ed. ***Who Got Einstein's Office? Eccentricity and Genius at the Institute for Advanced Study.*** Addison-Wesley, 1988. **1144** The Institute for Advanced Study provides the backdrop for this introduction to famous scientists, mathematicians, and their discoveries. The works of Albert Einstein, Kurt Gödel, and Richard Kuhn, among others, are examined by the author.	NFN	9–12	

	Type of literature	Grade span	Illus- trations

Richards, Norman. ***Dreamers and Doers: Inventors Who Changed Our World.*** Macmillan, 1984.

| | B | 6–12 | |

1145 The author introduces four American inventors—Robert Goddard, Charles Goodyear, Thomas Edison, and George Eastman—and discusses their lives and achievements.

Rius, Maria, and J. M. Parramon. ***The Four Elements: Air.*** Barron's, 1984.

| | NFI | K–3 | I |

1146 The author describes air with words that children can understand. This book is one of a series of four books (the others are *Fire, Water,* and *Earth*) that are also available in Spanish.

Rockwell, Anne. ***Trains.*** Dutton, 1988.

| | NFI | K–3 | I |

1147 All kinds of trains, from model trains to diesels, are described and illustrated.

Ross, Frank, Jr. ***Oracle Bones, Stars, and Wheelbarrows: Ancient Chinese Science and Technology.*** Houghton Mifflin, 1982.

| | NFI | 6–12 | |

1148 The author describes China's major scientific achievements and inventions. This book also includes glimpses of Chinese technology, civilization, and interaction with Western cultures.

Ross, Michael Elsohn. ***What Makes Everything Go?*** Yosemite, 1979.

| | NFI | 3–6 | I |

1149 The concept of energy is simply and engagingly presented.

Rutland, J. ***See Inside a Submarine.*** Franklin Watts, 1988.

| | NFI | 9–12 | I |

1150 The author highlights submarines by using cutaway drawings and photographs. [Technology]

Rybczynski, Witold. ***Taming the Tiger: The Struggle to Control Technology.*** Viking, 1985.

| | NFN | 9–12 | |

1151 The author comments on the dilemmas confronting humankind because of technology. He includes a historic perspective of this issue and suggests that one must keep in mind that it is we who control machines—not the converse. This book is not light reading. [Technology]

Salem, Lionel. ***Marvels of the Molecule.*** VCH, 1987.

| | NFI | 9–12 | |

1152 The author describes the formation and behavior of molecules. Although the concepts are complex, the illustrations and explanations make the book understandable and interesting.

Scarry, Huck. ***Balloon Trip: A Sketchbook.*** Prentice Hall, 1983.

| | NFI | 3–9 | S |

1153 The author's fascination with balloons is reflected in his discussion of their history, balloon parts, and the differences between using hydrogen and hot air for ballooning.

Schwartz, Joe. ***Einstein for Beginners.*** Pantheon, 1979.

| | NFI | 9–12 | I |

1154 Using a cartoon format, the author covers the early life of Albert Einstein and the scientific and social climate of his era. Also included are the development of the calculations for Einstein's theory of relativity and the formulas that he devised.

Seeger, Raymond. ***Benjamin Franklin: New World Physicist.*** Pergamon, 1973.

| | B | 9–12 | I |

1155 This book includes Benjamin Franklin's original papers that reveal his scientific and political thinking.

	Type of literature	Grade span	Illustrations
Silverstein, Alvin, and Virginia Silverstein. *Glasses and Contact Lenses: Your Guide to Eyes, Eyewear, and Eye Care.* Harper, 1989. **1156** This book covers the history of glasses, the eye's physical structure, types of vision problems, and the corrective measures currently available.	NFI	6–9	P
Simon, Seymour. *Soap Bubble Magic.* Lothrop, Lee and Shepard, 1985. **1157** This book contains more than just recipes for bigger and better bubbles. The author encourages scientific thinking by having students manipulate different variables. Topics such as air pressure, surface tension, and light refraction are delightfully presented.	NFI	K–6	I
Sleator, William. *Singularity.* Dutton, 1985. **1158** In this science fiction tale, twin brothers house-sit for their great-uncle. Adventures start because the house has a secret means of slowing and speeding time.	SF	6–12	
Songs from Unsung Worlds: Science in Poetry. Edited by Bonnie Bilyeau Gordon. Birkhäuser, 1985. **1159** This anthology of contemporary science-related poetry addresses the spirit and mystique of science. Many of the poems were written by well-known scientists. The biographical notes on the poets and scientists who contributed to this collection are also intriguing to read.	P	9–12	
Spielberg, Nathan, and Byron D. Anderson. *Seven Ideas That Shook the Universe.* John Wiley, 1985. **1160** The author explores the histories of seven important themes in physics: Copernican astronomy, Newtonian mechanics, energy and entropy, relativity, quantum theory, conservation principles, and symmetries. Together, these discoveries form the foundation of our understanding of the physical world.	NFI	9–12	
Stoll, Clifford. *The Cuckoo's Egg: Inside the World of Computer Espionage.* Doubleday, 1989. **1161** In this true account Clifford Stoll describes how he stumbled across and then systematically traced an international spy ring that cleverly used computer networks.	NFN	9–12	
Stone, A. Harris, and Bertram M. Siegel. *The Chemistry of Soap.* Prentice Hall, 1968. **1162** The chemical facets of soap are introduced in this book, which covers refraction, cohesion, properties of acids and bases, surface tension, and emulsion.	NFI	3–9	I
Tchudi, Stephen. *Probing the Unknown: From Myth to Science.* Macmillan, 1990. **1163** The author explains evolution from myth to science in a lively manner. He emphasizes logic and critical thinking. A "probing on your own" section encourages readers to test the validity of certain paradigms.	NFN	6–9	
Tchudi, Stephen. *Soda Poppery: The History of Soft Drinks in America.* Macmillan, 1986. **1164** The author covers the historical, social, and physical aspects involved in creating and consuming soft drinks in America.	NFI	9–12	I

	Type of literature	Grade span	Illus- trations

Trefil, James. *Scientist at the Seashore.* Macmillan, 1987. — NFI, 9–12

1165 This famous physicist uses a visit to the beach to explore topics and raise interesting questions. The individual chapters could stand on their own as stimuli for critical thinking on big questions.

Tucker, Wallace, and Karen Tucker. *The Dark Matter: The Quest for the Mass Hidden in Our Universe.* William Morrow, 1991. — NFI, 9–12, I

1166 While providing insight into the nature of scientific discovery and methods, this book offers information on those parts of our universe we can only measure.

Watson, Lyall. *The Dreams of Dragons.* William Morrow, 1987. — NFN, 9–12

1167 In this series of essays, the author writes on familiar topics, exploring unusual and little-known details.

Weinberg, Steven. *The First Three Minutes: A Modern View of the Origin of the Universe.* Basic Books, 1988. — NFI, 9–12

1168 This Nobel prize–winning physicist describes the events believed to have taken place during the first three minutes of the formation of the universe.

Weir, David. *The Bhopal Syndrome: Pesticides, Environment, and Health.* Sierra Club, 1987. — NFN, 9–12

1169 Eyewitness accounts document the environmental disaster in the city of Bhopal, India. The book then details potential hazards from the production and chronic misuse of pesticides. [Ecology] [Technology]

Weitzman, David. *Windmills, Bridges, and Old Machines: Discovering Our Industrial Past.* Macmillan, 1982. — NFI, 6–12, I

1170 The author describes the wonderful inventions, machines, and bridges that are part of America's past.

White, Jack R. *The Hidden World of Forces.* Putnam, 1987. — NFN, 6–12, I

1171 The author presents electromagnetism, gravitation, surface tension, friction, and other forces in the universe.

White, Laurence B., and Ray Broekel. *Optical Illusions.* Franklin Watts, 1986. — NFI, 6–12, I

1172 The author explores optical illusions and explains how they work. Many examples of different types of optical illusions are included.

Why in the World? National Geographic Society, 1985. — NFI, 3–9, P

1173 With the use of cartoons, quality pictures, and engaging prose, this book answers questions on a variety of topics without being encyclopedic.

Will, Clifford M. *Was Einstein Right? Putting General Relativity to the Test.* Basic Books, 1988. — NFN, 9–12

1174 Dramatic stories are told of experiments testing Einstein's predictions based on his theory of general relativity.

Wolfe, Tom. *The Right Stuff.* Bantam, 1983. — NFN, 9–12

1175 This first-person account of the early NASA manned rocket program includes its successes and failures and the people committed to the program. [Technology]

Type of literature	Grade span	Illus- trations
NFN	9–12	P
NFI	3–9	I
B	9–12	P

Wolf, Fred Alan. *Taking the Quantum Leap: The New Physics for Nonscientists.* Harper, 1989.

1176 This lively explanation of the ideas of quantum physics is presented in a style intended for nonphysicists. A thread of history and imaginative concepts runs throughout this narrative, inspiring mind-stretching visions.

Woods, Geraldine. *Science in Ancient Egypt.* Franklin Watts, 1988.

1177 This introduction to ancient Egyptian science and technology emphasizes this civilization's extensive use of practical mathematics, medical techniques, and craftsmanship.

Yeager, Chuck, and Leo Janos. *Yeager: An Autobiography.* Bantam, 1986.

1178 General Chuck Yeager discusses the secret of his success in this descriptive account of his life and career.

EARTH SCIENCES

The earth sciences are astronomy, geology, meteorology, and oceanography. *Anno's Sundial,* by Mitsumasa Anna, presents simple information about the movement of the sun and the earth. The history of life from millions of years ago is contained in narratives such as Aliki's *Digging Up Dinosaurs. Listen to the Rain,* by Bill Martin, Jr., and John Archambault, is a collection of poems about the weather. The study of the oceans is represented by books such as *Dove,* the biographical account of Robin Graham. John Baines's *Acid Rain* stresses the worldwide environmental effect of technology on atmospheric processes. The excitement and potential of the technology of spaceflight are conveyed in Sally Ride and Susan Okie's *To Space and Back.*

	Type of literature	Grade span	Illustrations
Aardema, Verna. ***Bringing the Rain to Kapiti Plain.*** Dial, 1981. **1179** In this rhythmic African folktale, Ki-pat shoots an arrow into large clouds, causing rain to fall and ending the drought. [Folklore] [Ecology]	NFN	3–6	I
Aliki. ***Digging Up Dinosaurs.*** Harper, 1988. **1180** Dinosaurs and fossils are introduced together with a team of experts who cooperate in their identification and reconstruction.	NFN	3–6	S
Aliki. ***Dinosaur Bones.*** Harper, 1990. **1181** This is a simple history of early scientific efforts to identify dinosaurs after their teeth were first found and identified in 1882.	NFN	K–3	I
Aliki. ***Fossils Tell of Long Ago.*** Harper, 1990. **1182** Various types of fossils are introduced and simple language is used to describe how the fossils were formed and what we have learned from studying them.	NFN	K–6	I
Allen, Joseph P. ***Entering Space: An Astronaut's Odyssey.*** Stewart, Tabori and Chang, 1984. **1183** This book provides accounts of living and working in space, including the exciting rescue of two nonfunctional satellites that were brought back to the planet Earth. [Technology]	NFN	9–12	P
Allison, Linda. ***The Reasons for Seasons.*** Little, Brown, 1975. **1184** Information about the four seasons is introduced. This book also includes projects, activities, and experiments.	NFI	3–9	I
Anno, Mitsumasa. ***Anno's Sundial.*** Putnam, 1987. **1185** This engaging pop-up book treats the reader to a three-dimensional view of time. Graphically, it simply and clearly shows the complex relationship between the motions of the sun and the earth.	NFI	6–12	S
Arnold, Caroline. ***Dinosaur Mountain: Graveyard of the Past.*** Ticknor and Fields, 1990. **1186** The discoveries made at the Dinosaur National Monument quarry in Utah are described, and the detailed work of paleontologists is highlighted.	NFI	K–6	P
Arnold, Caroline. ***Trapped in Tar: Fossils from the Ice Age.*** Ticknor and Fields, 1987. **1187** The La Brea tar pits in southern California are described, as are their value and importance to paleontologists who study Ice Age plants and animals.	NFI	3–9	P

	Type of literature	Grade span	Illustrations

Asimov, Isaac. *Far as Human Eye Could See.* Doubleday, 1987.
1188 This collection of essays was written for the lay person. The topics include physical chemistry, biochemistry, geochemistry, and astronomy.

	NFI	9–12	

Asimov, Isaac. *Young Extraterrestrials.* Harper, 1984.
1189 These science fiction short stories explore what life might be like for extraterrestrials who live on the planet Earth.

	SF	6–9	

Baines, John. *Acid Rain.* Steck-Vaughn, 1990.
1190 Acid rain's effects worldwide are described. A list of environmental organizations is also included. [Ecology] [Technology]

	NFI	9–12	I

Bakker, Robert T. *The Dinosaur Heresies: New Theories Unlocking the Mystery of the Dinosaurs and Their Extinction.* Zebra, 1988.
1191 A warm, thought-provoking book that introduces fascinating fossil animals very different from the stereotypical dinosaur.

	NFI	9–12	

Ballard, J. G. *The Drowned World.* Dent, 1983.
1192 In this science fiction novel people try to cope as conditions similar to the Triassic period develop.

	SF	9–12	

Ballard, Robert D. *Exploring the Titanic.* Edited by Patrick Crean. Scholastic, 1988.
1193 This story describes the sinking, eventual discovery, and exploration of the Titanic. [Technology]

	NFN	6–12	I

Balzola, Asun, and J. M. Parramon. *Spring.* Children's Press, 1981.
1194 The bold illustrations and simple text explain what happens in nature during spring. Other books in this series are *Autumn, Winter,* and *Summer.*

	F	K–3	I

Bannan, Jan Gumprecht. *Sand Dunes.* Carolrhoda, 1989.
1195 The formation of sand dunes and the natural forces that shape them are described in this photo-essay book. [Ecology]

	NFI	3–9	P

Baylor, Byrd. *Everybody Needs a Rock.* Aladdin, 1985.
1196 Independent thinking is valued and encouraged in this poem, which describes rules for selecting the perfect rock.

	NFN	K–6	I

Baylor, Byrd. *If You Are a Hunter of Fossils.* Aladdin, 1984.
1197 In this poem the author shares her love for hunting fossils and tells of the wonderful things that might be found by someone hunting for fossils.

	NFN	3–6	I

Beattie, Owen, and John Geiger. *Frozen in Time: Unlocking the Secrets of the Franklin Expedition.* Dutton, 1990.
1198 The disappearance of the Franklin arctic expedition, 1845–1848, is solved, and the cruel blow dealt to its members by scientists at that time is described.

	NFN	9–12	P

Bennett, David. *Day and Night.* Bantam, 1988.
1199 Simple explanations are given for the earth's rotation around the sun and the resulting cycle of the seasons.

	NFI	K–3	I

Bennett, David. *Earth.* Bantam, 1988.
1200 Earth's place in the solar system is explained, as are the different elements that make up our unique planet.

	NFI	K–3	I

	Type of literature	Grade span	Illus-trations
Bennett, David. *Rain.* Bantam, 1988. **1201** The simple text and bold illustrations follow a drop of rain through the water cycle and explain storms, thunder, and lightning.	NFI	K–3	I
Berger, Melvin. *Comets, Meteors, and Asteroids.* Putnam, 1981. **1202** Comets, meteors, and asteroids are shown in beautiful photographs and drawings that accompany clear explanations of their origins and appearance.	NFI	3–6	I
Berger, Melvin. *Star Gazing, Comet Tracking, and Sky Mapping.* Putnam, 1984. **1203** Naked-eye astronomy is introduced with star charts for 30 constellations, instructions for the best viewings, directions for making an astrolabe, and plans for astronomy projects.	NFI	6–9	I
Borden, Louise. *Caps, Hats, Socks, and Mittens: A Book About the Four Seasons.* Scholastic, 1989. **1204** Almost poetry, the narrative highlights the simple adventures children have each season.	F	K–3	I
Bova, Ben. *Welcome to Moon Base.* Ballantine, 1987. **1205** This takes the form of a science fiction handbook for living on the moon. [Technology]	SF	6–12	I
Branley, Franklyn M. *The Beginning of the Earth.* Harper, 1988. **1206** This book describes the processes the earth has gone through as oceans, mountains, and continents have been formed.	NFI	3–6	I
Branley, Franklyn M. *Comets.* Harper, 1987. **1207** The source and composition of comets are explained.	NFI	K–6	S
Branley, Franklyn M. *Earthquakes.* Harper, 1990. **1208** This book has basic information on earthquakes—their causes and effects—as well as instructions for self-protection during an earthquake.	NFI	K–6	I
Branley, Franklyn M. *Eclipse: Darkness in Daytime.* Harper, 1988. **1209** Solar eclipses are explained, and the history of their effects on ancient cultures is presented.	NFI	3–6	I
Branley, Franklyn M. *Flash, Crash, Rumble, and Roll.* Harper, 1985. **1210** Lightning and thunder are clearly explained, and safety tips to follow during storms are provided.	NFI	3–6	I
Branley, Franklyn M. *From Sputnik to Space Shuttles: Into the New Space Age.* Harper, 1986. **1211** This history of artificial satellites presents information on their importance to scientific advances and their value for experiments. [Technology]	NFI	3–9	I
Branley, Franklyn M. *It's Raining Cats and Dogs: All Kinds of Weather and Why We Have It.* Houghton Mifflin, 1987. **1212** This entertaining and informative book about weather explains wind, precipitation, smog, tornadoes, dust devils, and other related phenomena.	NFI	3–6	I
Branley, Franklyn M. *Journey into a Black Hole.* Harper, 1988. **1213** The concept of a black hole in space is described, as is the complex occurrence of the collapse and "death" of a star.	NFI	3–6	I

	Type of literature	Grade span	Illus-trations

Branley, Franklyn M. *The Moon Seems to Change.* Harper, 1987. — NFI — 3–6 — I

   1214 The moon's phases are explained, and hands-on experiments are described.

Branley, Franklyn M. *Saturn: The Spectacular Planet.* Harper, 1987. — NFI — 3–6 — P

   1215 Close-up photographs of Saturn were taken by the *Voyager 1* and *2* probes. The descriptions in this book include information about Saturn's physical features, characteristics, rings, and moons.

Branley, Franklyn M. *The Sky Is Full of Stars.* Harper, 1983. — NFI — 3–6 — I

   1216 The drawings and text focus on the brightest stars and constellations seen each season.

Branley, Franklyn M. *Sunshine Makes the Seasons.* Harper, 1988. — NFI — 3–6 — I

   1217 Seasonal changes are explained through the relationship of the earth to the sun and their respective orbits. A hands-on experiment helps clarify this concept.

Brin, David. *Startide Rising.* Bantam, 1984. — SF — 9–12

   1218 In this science fiction tale, a dolphin-commanded star ship from the planet Earth runs into trouble and hides in an alien ocean.

Bryan, C. D. *The National Air and Space Museum.* Harry Abrams, 1988. — NFI — 6–12 — P

   1219 This in-depth presentation of flight starts with the first attempts at flight and continues to current space flights. The pictures and illustrations are exceptional. [Technology]

Buck, Pearl S. *The Big Wave.* Harper, 1986. — F — 6–9

   1220 Jiya struggles to appreciate life and bravery and to overcome sorrow in this classic tale.

Carr, Terry. *Spill! The Story of the Exxon Valdez.* Franklin Watts, 1991. — NFN — 3–6 — P

   1221 The 1989 Alaskan oil spill is introduced, including its effects on wildlife, the ecosystem, and the economy. The color photographs depict the devastation, the problems encountered in cleaning the area, and the difficulties involved in saving wildlife. [Ecology] [Technology]

Carrick, Carol. *Big Old Bones: A Dinosaur Tale.* Ticknor and Fields, 1989. — NFN — K–3 — I

   1222 This humorous story tells about an early scientist who goes out West, finds bunches of bones, takes the bones home, and tries to reassemble them without knowing what dinosaurs were or how they might have looked. Information is included at the end of the book about scientific mix-ups that actually happened.

Carson, Rachel. *The Sea Around Us.* Oxford, 1991. — NFN — 9–12 — P

   1223 This classic describes the earth's oceans: their formations, histories, currents, and the flora and fauna that live in them.

Clarke, Arthur C. *The Deep Range.* Bantam, 1991. — SF — 9–12 — I

   1224 This science fiction action story traces the career change of a grounded spaceman who starts out as a whale herder and finally becomes Director of the Bureau of Whales. [Technology]

	Type of literature	Grade span	Illus- trations
Clarke, Arthur C. *Rendezvous with Rama.* Bantam, 1990. **1225** This classic science fiction story is about the planet Earth's first contact with aliens as Commander Norton and his crew explore an alien spaceship.	SF	9–12	
Cole, Joanna. *The Magic School Bus: At the Waterworks.* Scholastic, 1986. **1226** A city's waterworks system is introduced with an imaginary field trip on which the water cycle and each step taken to ensure a pure water supply are clearly described. [Technology]	NFN	K–6	I
Cole, Joanna. *The Magic School Bus: Inside the Earth.* Scholastic, 1989. **1227** Humor and an imaginary field trip make it easy to learn about rocks and the earth. This book includes information about the formation of rocks, rock layers, uses for rocks, and rock collections.	NFN	K–6	I
Cole, Joanna. *The Magic School Bus: Lost in the Solar System.* Scholastic, 1990. **1228** In a fantastical field trip through the solar system, many facts are presented in a clever and humorous manner as the school bus travels past the sun and around the planets.	NFN	K–6	I
Cole, Sheila. *When the Tide Is Low.* Lothrop, Lee and Shepard, 1985. **1229** A mother tells her daughter about the plants and animals they will find on the seashore during low tide.	F	K–3	I
Cousteau, Jacques-Yves, and Philippe Diolé. *Three Adventures: Galápagos, Titicaca, The Blue Holes.* Doubleday, 1973. **1230** Cousteau describes three undersea adventures and discusses the plants, animals, and environments of the Galápagos Islands, Lake Titicaca, and the Blue Holes. [Ecology]	F	K–6	I
Cross, Wilbur. *Petroleum.* Children's Press, 1983. **1231** This introduction to the petroleum industry begins with information on the research necessary to locate oil and continues through the processes necessary to develop usable petroleum. [Technology]	NFI	6–12	
Dancing Teepees: Poems of American Indian Youth. Edited by Virginia Sneve. Holiday House, 1989. **1232** Sneve selected for this collection both historical oral poems and poems by contemporary North American Indians.	P	6–9	I
Darling, David J. *The Moon: A Spaceflight Away.** Dillon Press, 1984. **1233** The moon is introduced with current information and facts.	NFI	3–9	P
Darling, David J. *The New Astronomy: An Ever-Changing Universe.* Macmillan, 1985. **1234** This book introduces the instruments used to study both astronomy and electromagnetic radiation.	NFI	3–9	
Darling, David J. *The Stars: From Birth to Black Hole.* Dillon Press, 1987. **1235** Stars are discussed in detail: their types, composition, sizes, ages, weights, changes, and explosions.	NFI	3–9	P

	Type of literature	Grade span	Illustrations
Darling, David J. *The Sun: Our Neighborhood Star.** Dillon Press, 1984. **1236** Our sun is defined and its importance to life on earth is described. Explanations in this book cover orbits, weather, and energy.	NFI	3–9	I
Darling, David J. *The Universe: Past, Present, and Future.* Macmillan, 1985. **1237** The author presents the current theories about the formation and origin of space.	NFI	3–9	P
Darling, David J. *Where Are We Going in Space?* Macmillan, 1984. **1238** The author discusses our solar system and possibilities for its exploration.	NFI	3–6	P
De Paola, Tomie. *The Cloud Book.* Holiday House, 1975. **1239** Clouds are identified by both their common and their scientific names and are compared to familiar objects.	NFN	K–3	I
De Paola, Tomie. *The Quicksand Book.* Holiday House, 1977. **1240** The composition of quicksand is described in this book that includes safety precautions, rescue procedures, and a recipe for making quicksand.	NFN	K–3	I
Dorros, Arthur. *Feel the Wind.* Harper, 1990. **1241** The author uses simple terms to explain air currents, define the weather terms for wind, and describe uses of wind.	NFN	K–3	I
Embury, Barbara, and Tom D. Crouch. *The Dream Is Alive: A Flight of Discovery Aboard the Space Shuttle.* Harper, 1990. **1242** Three 1984 space shuttle flights are documented with color photographs and a text that includes the history of rockets, biographical sketches of the crew members, diagrams of the launchers and crews' cabins, and the crews' equipment and clothing.	NFN	6–9	P
Ferris, Jeri. *Arctic Explorer: The Story of Matthew Henson.* Carolrhoda, 1989. **1243** This is the biography of the black man who accompanied Admiral Peary on four polar expeditions. It provides information on their scientific discoveries, life in the Arctic, and the Eskimos' customs.	B	9–12	P
Ferris, Timothy. *Coming of Age in the Milky Way.* Doubleday, 1989. **1244** Ferris traces the development of our perceptions of the "heavens"— from ancient to modern times. In a lively style, the author clarifies the physical laws governing the universe.	NFN	6–12	P
Ferris, Timothy. *Galaxies.* Stewart, Tabori and Chang, 1982. **1245** This oversize book has beautiful photographs and drawings and a four-page foldout of the Milky Way. The author weaves facts and history as he takes readers on a hypothetical expedition through the universe.	NFI	6–12	P
Ferris, Timothy. *Spaceshots: The Beauty of Nature Beyond Earth.* Pantheon, 1984. **1246** This book has extraordinary photographs of planets, stars, galaxies, auroras, shooting stars, and eclipses, with detailed explanations of the equipment used to take these photographs.	NFI	6–12	P

	Type of literature	Grade span	Illustrations

First Contact: The Search for Extraterrestrial Intelligence.
Edited by Ben Bova and Byron Preiss. Dutton, 1990.
1247 Scientists involved in the Search for Extraterrestrial Intelligence Program explain their theories and their work. [Technology] — NFN, 9–12

Fisher, David E. *The Origin and Evolution of Our Own Particular Universe.* Atheneum, 1988.
1248 This engaging book explores the growth of man's scientific knowledge about the universe, especially the formation of our planet and solar system. — NFN, 9–12

Florian, Douglas. *A Winter Day.* Greenwillow, 1987.
1249 This simple picture book illustrates a family's winter activities, both indoors and outdoors. — NFN, K–3, I

Foster, Janet. *Journey to the Top of the World.* Prentice Hall, 1988.
1250 This story is about a journey across the Canadian Arctic and shows both the natural history and the extensive animal life found there. — NFN, 6–12, P

Fradin, Dennis B. *The Voyager Space Probes.* Children's Press, 1985.
1251 This pictorial essay of the United States's *Voyager* probes to the outer planets includes photographs sent back to earth from the spacecrafts. [Technology] — NFI, 3–6, P

Gallant, Ray A. *Our Restless Earth.* Franklin Watts, 1986.
1252 This book discusses the conclusions geologists have reached about the formation of the planet Earth and the evidence that explains the changes that have occurred. — NFI, 6–9, I

Gallant, Roy A. *Our Universe.* National Geographic Society, 1980.
1253 This National Geographic picture atlas of our universe has many beautiful pictures. — NFI, 3–9, I

Gallant, Roy A. *The Private Lives of the Stars.* Macmillan, 1986.
1254 This book describes the dangers of being an astronomer in ancient times as well as the stargazing activities of early cultures. Current knowledge of stars, their characteristics and classifications, is also presented. — NFI, 9–12

Gallant, Roy A. *Rainbows, Mirages, and Sundogs: The Sky as a Source of Wonder.* Macmillan, 1987.
1255 This delightful book explains and discusses the visual phenomena in the sky and the interactions of light and atmosphere that cause these phenomena. The drawings and illustrations are helpful in explaining the concepts involved. — NFI, 6–9, I

Gans, Roma. *Rock Collecting.* Harper, 1984.
1256 The author gives simple suggestions for starting, organizing, and enjoying a rock collection. Also included is information on the history, types, and uses of rocks. — NFI, 3–6, I

Gibbons, Gail. *Sun Up, Sun Down.* Harcourt Brace Jovanovich, 1987.
1257 The narrator, a little girl, tells about the sun, the clouds that produce rain, and the rainbows that are produced as the sun shines through raindrops. — NFI, K–3, I

Gibbons, Gail. *Weather Forecasting.* Four Winds, 1987.
1258 The author explains why weather is studied, defines the terms used to describe weather, and discusses the people and equipment needed for tracking and gauging weather's constant changes. [Technology] — NFI, 3–6, I

	Type of literature	Grade span	Illus- trations

Gibbons, Gail. *Weather Words and What They Mean.* Holiday House, 1990.

1259 This book clearly defines the factors that influence weather and the terms used to describe different types of weather.

NFI	K–6	I

Gilman, Michael. *Matthew Henson: Explorer.* Holloway, 1990.

1260 This biography introduces Henson, Admiral Peary's friend and assistant, and describes their arrival at the North Pole and their many adventures exploring the Arctic Circle.

B	6–9	

Goldsmith, Donald. *Supernova: The Exploding Star of 1987.* St. Martin's, 1989.

1261 The discovery and observation in 1987 of a giant supernova is described, and its importance to our understanding of the universe emphasized.

NFI	6–12	I

Graham, Robin Lee, and Derek Gill. *Dove.* Harper, 1991.

1262 This book highlights sixteen-year-old Robin's solo voyage around the world in the 24-foot sloop *Dove.* His ability to use maps, instruments, and common sense helps him meet nature's challenges.

B	6–12	

Hackwell, W. John. *Digging to the Past: Excavations in Ancient Lands.* Scribner's, 1986.

1263 This book describes aspects of an archaeological dig, details the roles of the technical team, and highlights the daily routines and difficulties.

NFI	6–9	I

Harrington, John W. *Dance of the Continents: Adventures with Rocks and Time.* Tarcher, 1983.

1264 Harrington weaves the past with the present in these discourses on geology. By blending poetry with theory he accomplishes the incredible feat of imparting large quantities of scientific knowledge.

NFI	6–12	I

Heinlein, Robert A. *The Moon Is a Harsh Mistress.* Ace, 1987.

1265 In this classic science fiction tale, a computer helps the moon colonists win their battle for independence from the planet Earth.

SF	9–12	

Hendershot, Judith. *In Coal Country.* Edited by Frances Foster. Knopf, 1987.

1266 A child describes growing up in a coal-mining community.

NFN	3–6	I

Heyerdahl, Thor. *Easter Island.* Random House, 1989.

1267 The author describes drifting from South America across the Pacific Ocean to Easter Island in a raft. He then describes his observations of Easter Island.

NFN	9–12	P

Heyerdahl, Thor. *Kon-Tiki.* Simon and Schuster, 1987.

1268 The author describes traveling by raft across the Pacific Ocean from Tahiti to Hawaii.

NFN	9–12	P

Hines, Anna G. *Sky All Around.* Houghton Mifflin, 1989.

1269 In this simple story a father and daughter enjoy identifying stars in the night sky. They look forward to sharing their knowledge with other family members.

NFN	K–3	I

	Type of literature	Grade span	Illus-trations
Hirst, Robin, and Sally Hirst. *My Place in Space.* Orchard Books, 1990. **1270** In this delightful, humorous book, Henry gives a specific, exact, and detailed description of his home's location on Main Street, in the Southern Hemisphere, on the planet Earth, and so on through the solar system.	NFN	K–6	I
Hiscock, Bruce. *The Big Rock.* Macmillan, 1988. **1271** This book traces the origins of a granite rock located near the mountains and explains how it reveals information about the history of the earth.	NFN	K–6	I
Hiscock, Bruce. *Tundra: The Arctic Land.* Macmillan, 1986. **1272** This book describes the tundra and explains how organisms adapt to its harsh conditions. [Ecology]	NFN	3–9	I
Hodges, Margaret. *The Wave.* Houghton Mifflin, 1964. **1273** In this story a Japanese farmer burns his rice field to warn the other villagers that a tidal wave is approaching. [Folklore]	NFN	3–6	I
Hoff, Mary, and Mary M. Rodgers. *Our Endangered Planet: Groundwater.* Lerner, 1991. **1274** This book discusses groundwater's importance throughout the world and explains that much of it is polluted. [Ecology]	NFI	3–9	P
Hoff, Mary, and Mary M. Rodgers. *Our Endangered Planet: Rivers and Lakes.* Lerner, 1991. **1275** This book shows how rivers and lakes have been harmed by worldwide pollution and explains what must be done to save them. [Ecology]	NFI	3–9	P
Hopkins, Lee B. *Dinosaurs.* Harcourt Brace Jovanovich, 1990. **1276** Ink drawings illustrate poems about dinosaurs.	P	3–9	I
Hopkins, Lee B. *The Sky Is Full of Song.* Harper, 1987. **1277** This collection of short, lighthearted poems commemorate events of each season.	P	K–3	I
Horner, John K., and James Gorman. *Digging Dinosaurs.* Harper, 1990. **1278** In this captivating book the scientist who discovered the first nest of dinosaurs tells how he predicted, located, and excavated the maiasaurs' nesting grounds.	NFN	9–12	P
Hyde, Philip. *Drylands: The Deserts of North America.* Harcourt Brace Jovanovich, 1987. **1279** An oversize book with gorgeous photographs and a descriptive text introduce the flora, fauna, and geology of the five North American deserts. [Ecology]	NFN	9–12	P
Jacobs, Una. *Earth Calendar.* Silver Burdett, 1986. **1280** The author provides a comprehensive look at earth—its structure, climate, seasons—and discusses the interrelationship of the food and mineral cycles. The detailed color illustrations enhance the text and make the concepts easy to understand.	NFI	K–6	I
Jacobs, Una. *Sun Calendar.* Silver Burdett, 1986. **1281** This book explains the importance of sunlight for life on earth. The seasonal relationships are shown for the life patterns of plants, animals, insects, and people.	NFN	3–9	I

	Type of literature	Grade span	Illus-trations
Johanson, Donald, and Kevin O'Farrell. *Journey from the Dawn: Life with the World's First Family.* Random House, 1990. **1282** Anthropologist Johanson imagines early man's daily life three million years ago, producing a tantalizing picture of what our earliest ancestors may have been like and how they lived.	NFN	6–12	I
Johnson, Sylvia A. *Coral Reefs.* Lerner, 1984. **1283** This book introduces in detail the various kinds of coral reefs, their composition, and the marine life they support.	NFI	3–9	P
Kandoian, Ellen. *Under the Sun.* Putnam, 1990. **1284** A mother explains to her small daughter how night and day occur around the world.	NFN	K–3	I
Kelsey, Larry, and Darrell Hoff. *Recent Revolutions in Astronomy.* Franklin Watts, 1987. **1285** This book describes the recent work and research of astronomers.	NFI	6–12	S
Kent, Zachary. *The Story of the Challenger Disaster.* Children's Press, 1986. **1286** This brief account of the *Challenger* space shuttle tragedy includes information about each crew member. [Technology]	NFI	3–6	P
Krakel, Dean. *Downriver: A Yellowstone Journey.* Sierra Club Books, 1987. **1287** This journal is a description and history of the Yellowstone River Valley's ecosystem.	NFN	9–12	
Krupp, E. C. *The Big Dipper and You.* William Morrow, 1989. **1288** This book discusses the history, location, importance, and value of the Big Dipper to all cultures. The clever illustrations include guides for locating the Big Dipper and using it to find the North Star.	NFN	3–6	I
Krupp, E. C. *The Comet and You.* Macmillan, 1985. **1289** Witty and clever illustrations enhance this discussion of comets that includes facts about their compositions, orbits, speeds, and histories. This book also provides specific information about Halley's comet.	NFI	K–6	I
Lambert, David, and Ralph Hardy. *Weather and Its Work.* Facts on File, 1985. **1290** This is an informative book on global weather and the related phenomena that influence it. The explanations of the various climatic conditions are enhanced with superb photographs.	NFI	6–12	P
Lampton, Christopher. *New Theories on the Birth of the Universe.* Franklin Watts, 1989. **1291** This book has interesting discussions on how the universe began, how we know how it began, and how big it is.	NFI	9–12	
Larrick, Nancy. *When the Dark Comes Dancing: A Bedtime Poetry Book.* Putnam, 1983. **1292** This is a collection of traditional poems, from many cultures, that relate to nature.	P	K–3	I

	Type of literature	Grade span	Illus-trations

Lasky, Kathryn. *The Bone Wars.* Puffin, 1989.

    1293 This historical novel is set in the mid–1870s. When Thad Longworth becomes a scout for paleontologists searching for dinosaur fossils, he becomes involved in the rivalry between two groups of paleontologists.

(F, 6–9)

Lasky, Kathryn. *Dinosaur Dig.* William Morrow, 1990.

    1294 This book provides information about dinosaurs and details of the scientific procedures involved in an archaeological dig. It is written from the viewpoint of the members of a young family who join a dig in progress.

(NFN, 6–9, P)

Lauber, Patricia. *Dinosaurs Walked Here: And Other Stories Fossils Tell.* Aladdin, 1992.

    1295 This book introduces plant and animal fossils and the knowledge scientists gain of both the prehistoric world and today's world.

(NFI, 3–6, P)

Lauber, Patricia. *Journey to the Planets.* Crown Publishers, 1990.

    1296 Much of the information in this book is about the planets and moons in our solar system.

(NFI, 3–9, P)

Lauber, Patricia. *Meteors and Meteorites: Voyagers from Space.* Crowell, 1989.

    1297 This book addresses current scientific thinking about meteorites as clues to the origins of the solar system, explaining where meteors come from, how they were formed, and their effects on earth.

(NFN, 6–12, P)

Lauber, Patricia. *Seeing Earth from Space.* Orchard Books, 1990.

    1298 Stunning color photographs of earth taken from space encourage an awareness of global unity and the need to protect the planet. While describing how scientists study earth, Lauber also encourages ecological awareness. [Ecology]

(NFI, 3–9, P)

Lauber, Patricia. *Volcano: The Eruption and Healing of Mount St. Helens.* Bradbury, 1986.

    1299 This is the story of the eruption of the Mount St. Helens volcano. It includes the scientists' predictions of when the volcano would erupt, their observations of the eruption, and their surveillance of the returning plant and animal life.

(NFI, 3–6, P)

Leutscher, Alfred. *Water.* Dial, 1983.

    1300 This book highlights the power and beauty of water in its many forms and stresses that without it there would be no life.

(NFN, 3–6, I)

Lewis, Thomas P. *Hill of Fire.* Harper, 1971.

    1301 A story based on the 1943 eruption of the Paricutin volcano that describes the beginning of the eruption, the changes to the land, and the changes in Mexican villagers' lives.

(F, 3–6, I)

Livingston, Myra Cohn. *Space Songs.* Holiday House, 1988.

    1302 This poetry collection, with its imaginative illustrations and creative printing, describes a variety of spheres in space.

(P, 3–9, I)

Lloyd, David. *Air.* Dial, 1982.

    1303 This book discusses the positive uses of air, its destructive potential, and the problems caused by dirty air.

(NFN, K–6, I)

	Type of literature	Grade span	Illustrations
Locker, Thomas. *Where the River Begins.* Dial, 1984. **1304** Two boys and their grandfather follow the river they love to its headwaters. The landscape along the meandering river is beautifully illustrated.	F	3–6	I
Lowery, Linda. *Earth Day.* Carolrhoda, 1991. **1305** The history, meaning, and value of Earth Day is explained, and its celebrations around the world are described in this simple book.	NFN	K–3	I
Macaulay, David. *The Motel of the Mysteries.* Houghton Mifflin, 1979. **1306** The author takes a tongue-in-cheek look at how modern life might be erroneously interpreted by future scientists who try to study this century.	F	6–12	I
McNulty, Faith. *How to Dig a Hole to the Other Side of the World.* Harper, 1990. **1307** As a boy digs a hole to China, the interesting substances and layers he finds between the earth's surface and its core are described and colorfully illustrated in this classic book.	NFN	3–6	I
McPherson, Stephanie Sammartino. *Rooftop Astronomer: A Story About Maria Mitchell.* Carolrhoda, 1990. **1308** This biography is an introduction to Maria Mitchell, her love of astronomy, her research, and her unusual accomplishments in the belief that women deserved the same opportunities for an education that men enjoyed.	B	4–6	I
Maddern, Eric. *Earth Story.* Barron's, 1988. **1309** The formation of both the galaxy and earth itself is described in this book.	NFN	K–6	I
Madson, Chris. *When Nature Heals: The Greening of the Rock Mountain Arsenal.* Holt, Rinehart and Winston, 1990. **1310** The author describes a former pesticide manufacturing plant that has become one of the most significant wildlife refuges in the country. [Ecology]	NFI	6–12	P
Marston, Elsa. *Mysteries in American Archaeology.* Walker and Company, 1986. **1311** The author explores the mysteries of the structures left by early cultures. He also discusses the debate concerning when people crossed the Bering Strait to what is now North America.	NFI	6–12	
Martin, Bill, Jr., and John Archambault. *Listen to the Rain.* Holt, Rinehart and Winston, 1988. **1312** This poetry book introduces the sights and sounds of rain using very descriptive words and lovely illustrations.	P	K–3	I
Maurer, Richard. *Junk in Space.* Simon and Schuster, 1989. **1313** The cosmic garbage recently left in space is described and illustrated in this interesting book.	NFI	6–9	P
Mayne, William. *Earthfasts.* Dutton, 1966. **1314** In this science fiction tale an eighteenth-century drummer boy marches into the twentieth century. The two young main characters use scientific reasoning to understand what is happening and to set their world right again.	SF	6–12	

	Type of literature	Grade span	Illus-trations
Miller, Christina, and Louise Berry. **Wastes.** Franklin Watts, 1986. **1315** The author defines the terms used for wastes, looks at the history of garbage disposal, and discusses current methods for disposing of solid waste and sewage. [Ecology]	NFI	6–12	P
Miller, Walter. **A Canticle for Leibowitz.** Bantam, 1984. **1316** This science fiction tale is about a nuclear technician who witnesses a renaissance after World War III.	SF	9–12	
Mitgutsch, Ali. **From Swamp to Coal.** Carolrhoda, 1985. **1317** Coal is simply defined and described in this book, which includes illustrations of swamps, mines, coal processing, and the many uses for coal.	NFI	3–6	I
Monroe, Jean Guard, and Ray A. Williamson. **They Dance in the Sky: Native American Star Myths.** Houghton Mifflin, 1987. **1318** This is a collection of North American Indian legends that interpret astronomical phenomena. [Folklore]	NFN	3–6	I
Morrison, Lillian. **Overheard in a Bubble Chamber: And Other Science Poems.** Lothrop, Lee and Shepard, 1981. **1319** This poetry collection for the twenty-first century includes poems on natural history, mathematical measures, physical properties, heavenly bodies, and time.	P	9–12	
Moskin, Marietta D. **Sky Dragons and Flaming Swords: The Story of Eclipses, Comets, and Other Strange Happenings in the Skies.** Walker and Company, 1985. **1320** Astronomical phenomena are explained with both myths and legends as well as current knowledge that allows astronomers to predict eclipses, meteors, and comets.	NFN	3–6	P
Muir, John. **My First Summer in the Sierra.** Sierra Club Books, 1990. **1321** John Muir's vivid, lively descriptions convey the beauty of California's Sierra Nevada mountain range. [Ecology]	B	9–12	P
Niven, Larry. **Ringworld.** Ballantine, 1989. **1322** This science fiction tale follows a mixed human and alien team as they explore a huge hoop-shaped object that completely encircles a star.	SF	9–12	
Niven, Larry, and Jerry Pournelle. **Lucifer's Hammer.** Fawcett, 1985. **1323** This science fiction tale is about people whose lives are entwined as they face an approaching comet that will destroy their world. [Ecology]	SF	9–12	
North, Rick. **The Young Astronauts** (Number 1). Zebra, 1990. **1324** In this science fiction tale, the children in Nathan's group, considered troublesome, face their ultimate test: those who pass the Survival Trek are going to Mars. See also the sequels: *The Young Astronauts*, numbers 2–6.	SF	6–9	
O'Connor, Karen. **Garbage: Our Endangered Planet.** Lucent, 1989. **1325** This book examines our throw-away society, disposal sites, and the special problems of plastic trash in space. [Ecology]	NFI	6–12	P
Ostmann, Robert. **Acid Rain: A Plague upon the Waters.*** Dillon Press, 1982. **1326** Using the scientific evidence collected to date, the author traces the causes and effects of acid precipitation worldwide. [Ecology]	NFI	6–9	I

	Type of literature	Grade span	Illus-trations
Panati, Charles. *Extraordinary Origins of Everyday Things.* Harper, 1987. **1327** The author details the historical origins of everyday things from a human perspective.	NFI	6–12	I
Pearson, Susan. *My Favorite Time of Year.* Harper, 1988. **1328** A little girl delights in describing the special events each season brings.	F	K–3	I
Peters, Lisa Westberg. *The Sun, the Wind, and the Rain.* Holt, Rinehart and Winston, 1988. **1329** The author uses a little girl's sand mountain to explain the formation of mountains and their erosion from the elements. The colorful illustrations clarify the concepts introduced in this book.	NFN	K–6	I
Peters, Lisa Westberg. *Water's Way.* Little, Brown, 1991. **1330** In this simple story a young boy observes and learns about water's different forms and observes how water changes. The colorful illustrations clarify the concepts introduced in this book.	NFN	K–6	I
Polacco, Patricia. *Meteor!* Putnam, 1987. **1331** The author describes a meteorite falling in her grandparents' backyard and the chain of events this event causes.	NFN	K–3	I
Polacco, Patricia. *Thunder Cake.* Putnam, 1990. **1332** Using mathematics to calculate the distance of an approaching storm, a grandmother helps her granddaughter overcome her fear of thunder by counting and by making a cake.	F	K–3	I
Pringle, Laurence. *Rain of Troubles: The Science and Politics of Acid Rain.* Macmillan Children's Book Group, 1988. **1333** The author describes the effects of acid rain on the land, air, and waters of the United States and Canada. He also discusses the politics behind the failure to control the causes of acid rain and the technology being used to combat its negative effects on the environment. [Ecology]	NFI	6–12	I
Provensen, Alice, and Martin Provensen. *The Year at Maple Hill Farm.* Aladdin, 1988. **1334** This book describes monthly changes on a farm, especially as the seasons affect specific animals. [Ecology]	NFN	K–3	I
Provensen, Alice, and Martin Provensen. *A Book of Seasons.* Random House, 1976. **1335** Colorful, cheerful illustrations and short, simple sentences describe the passing of the seasons in a way that clarifies the difficult concept of a year to young children.	NFN	K 3	I
Provensen, Alice, and Martin Provensen. *The Glorious Flight Across the Channel with Louis Bleriot.* Puffin, 1987. **1336** This is a humorous story describing Louis Bleriot's persistence in developing seven airplanes before he became the first man to fly across the English Channel. [Technology]	NFN	3–6	I
Radlauer, Ruth, and Carolyn Young. *Voyagers One and Two: Robots in Space.* Children's Press, 1987. **1337** This book describing the *Voyager* spacecraft projects, instruments, and encounters was written before the project to Neptune. [Technology]	NFI	6–9	P

	Type of literature	Grade span	Illus-trations

Ride, Sally, and Susan Okie. *To Space and Back.* William Morrow, 1991.   **B**   6–9   P
1338 Color photographs and illustrations enhance Sally Ride's descriptions of the space shuttle, the launch, orbit, views of space, experiments, and the return to earth. [Technology]

Ritchie, David. *The Ring of Fire.* Simon and Schuster, 1981.   **NFI**   6–12
1339 The author introduces the volcanoes that form a ring around the Pacific Ocean.

Ritchie, David. *Superquake: Why Earthquakes Occur and When the Big One Will Hit Southern California.* Crown, 1988.   **NFI**   9–12
1340 The author describes an earthquake's patterns, components, and effects, including a vivid description of a big California earthquake.

Rossbacher, Lisa A. *Recent Revolutions in Geology.* Franklin Watts, 1986.   **NFI**   6–12
1341 This book covers recent discoveries on the earth and delves into the geology of the planets and other parts of our solar system. The author explains plate tectonics, volcanoes, and earthquakes.

Ruckman, Ivy. *Night of the Twisters.* Harper, 1986.   **F**   3–9
1342 This is a fictionalized account of the tornadoes that devastated Grand Island, Nebraska. The author provides additional information on the causes, force, and destructive power of tornadoes. She describes how both individuals and public agencies might prepare for and respond to disasters.

Sagan, Carl. *Contact.* Simon and Schuster, 1985.   **SF**   9–12
1343 In this science fiction story, Eleanor Arroway is a brilliant physicist who heads the team listening for a signal from an outer space project. When the message arrives, scientists mobilize their efforts to decode and respond to this message.

Sagan, Carl. *Cosmos.* Ballantine, 1985.   **NFN**   9–12   P
1344 This is a unique view of the science of astronomy, including its philosophical and historical foundations. The author stresses that human life constitutes a small part of life on earth and that we must use our knowledge wisely to protect the earth.

Sattler, Helen R. *Baby Dinosaurs.* Lothrop, Lee and Shepard, 1984.   **NFI**   3–6   I
1345 The author describes the nests, the eggs, the young, and their needs for protection. Her information is based on the fossilized remains of baby dinosaurs that have been found around the world.

Sattler, Helen R. *Dinosaurs of North America.* Lothrop, Lee and Shepard, 1981.   **NFI**   3–6   I
1346 The 80 varieties of dinosaurs that lived in North America are described, discussed, and illustrated in this book.

Schulke, Flip, and others. *Your Future in Space: The United States Space Camp Training Program.* Crown Publishers, 1986.   **NFN**   6–12   P
1347 This is an introduction to the Space Camp program in Huntsville, Alabama. The authors address living and working in space, gravity, mission training, and future projects. [Technology]

	Type of literature	Grade span	Illustrations
Seff, Philip, and Nancy R. Seff. *Our Fascinating Earth.* Contemporary Books, 1990. **1348** Anecdotes in this book are drawn from almost every scientific discipline, proving that science can be more unbelievable than science fiction.	NFN	9–12	I
Siebert, Diane. *Mojave.* Harper, 1988. **1349** Using the beautiful, figurative language of poetry and striking, bold illustrations, this book describes the natural life and the everchanging features of America's great Mojave Desert.	P	3–6	I
Simon, Seymour. *Galaxies.* William Morrow, 1991. **1350** Magnificent photographs from the National Optical Astronomy observatories reinforce a text that explains the known facts about galaxies.	NFI	3–9	P
Simon, Seymour. *Icebergs and Glaciers.* William Morrow, 1987. **1351** Panoramic color photographs enhance a text that follows the development of glaciers and icebergs from a single snowflake.	NFI	3–9	P
Simon, Seymour. *Jupiter.* William Morrow, 1988. **1352** Color photographs and illustrations enhance this introduction to Jupiter and its moons. Other books to see in this series include *Saturn, Mars,* and *Uranus.*	NFI	3–9	P
Simon, Seymour. *The Long Journey from Space.* Crown Publishers, 1982. **1353** This is a colorful introduction to the history and nature of comets and meteors.	NFI	3–9	P
Simon, Seymour. *The Long View into Space.* Crown Publishers, 1987. **1354** This is a photographic space journey from earth to the moon, the sun, the stars in our solar system, and other galaxies. The relationships of our solar system to other galaxies is clarified by the author. Other books in this series include *The Sun* and *The Moon.*	NFI	3–9	P
Simon, Seymour. *Look to the Night Sky.* Puffin, 1979. **1355** This primer for stargazing, which includes an overview of the night sky, discusses the hourly drift of the stars, the seasonal progression of constellations, and the problems of light pollution.	NFI	3–9	P
Simon, Seymour. *Oceans.* William Morrow, 1990. **1356** The author looks at the distribution of water across the planet, the nature of waves, and the tides and their effects on the land. The spectacular photographs highlight a text that stresses global interdependence.	NFI	3–9	P
Simon, Seymour. *Stars.* William Morrow, 1986. **1357** Color photographs and illustrations highlight the formations, locations, aging, and disappearances of stars.	NFI	3–9	P
Simon, Seymour. *Storms.* William Morrow, 1989. **1358** The author describes the atmospheric conditions that create storms and discusses the value and importance of storms in maintaining the world's climate.	NFI	3–9	P

	Type of literature	Grade span	Illus-trations
Simon, Seymour. *Volcanoes.* William Morrow, 1988. **1359** Shield, cinder cone, composite, and dome volcanoes are presented in this introduction that has color photographs of well-known volcanoes and their recent eruptions. Another book to see in this series is *Earthquakes.*	NFI	3–9	P
Smucker, Anna Egan. *No Star Nights.* Knopf, 1989. **1360** A little girl describes growing up in a mill town with dust and pollution. She tells about never seeing the night sky because of the red glow from the furnaces. Finally, she describes the area after the mill and the young families have left.	F	K–6	I
Sperry, Armstrong. *Call It Courage.* Aladdin, 1990. **1361** As Mafatu struggles to survive alone on a coral reef, he remembers happier days and the seafaring life of his Polynesian culture. [Ecology]	F	3–9	
Steger, Will, and Jon Bowermaster. *Saving the Earth: A Citizen's Guide to Environmental Action.* Knopf, 1990. **1362** Earth's most pressing ecological problems are discussed by the authors, who address issues regarding atmosphere, land, water, and people. Also included is a list of environmental and world relief organizations. [Ecology]	NFI	9–12	I
Symes, R. F., and others. *Rocks and Minerals.* Knopf, 1988. **1363** This book is an extensive introduction to rocks and minerals. Precise, detailed photographs supplement a text that will intrigue and fascinate any reader.	NFI	3–9	P
Taylor, Theodore. *The Cay.* Avon, 1991. **1364** In this survival, adventure story, a blind white boy and an old black man are shipwrecked on a Caribbean island.	F	6–9	
Torres, George. *Space Shuttle: A Quantum Leap.* Presidio Books, 1986. **1365** This is an overview of past, present, and possible future endeavors in the space program. The author charts the early space missions and discusses the military use of space, manufacturing for the space program, and scientific space exploration.	NFN	6–12	P
Trefil, James. *Meditations at 10,000 Feet: A Scientist in the Mountains.* Macmillan, 1987. **1366** This collection of geological topics makes intriguing reading.	NFI	9–12	
Van Allsburg, Chris. *Just a Dream.* Houghton Mifflin, 1990. **1367** A thoughtless boy dreams about a garbage-covered world and then resolves to make an effort to improve the environment.	F	3–6	I
Vare, Ehtlie, and Greg Ptacek. *Mothers of Invention: From the Bra to the Bomb, Forgotten Women and Their Unforgettable Ideas.* William Morrow, 1987. **1368** Women inventors are the focus of this book. The brief entries describe these inventors and their inventions.	NFN	6–12	I
Vendrell, Carme Sole. *Earth.* Barron's, 1985. **1369** The simple text describes the planet Earth for young children. (Available in Spanish)	NFN	K–3	I

	Type of literature	Grade span	Illustrations

Vendrell, Carme Sole. *Water.* Barron's, 1985.

1370 This easy book gives children a sense of the locations and importance of water. (Available in Spanish)

| | NFN | K–3 | I |

Verne, Jules. *A Journey to the Center of the Earth.* Dutton, 1986.

1371 In this classic science fiction tale, Professor von Hardwigg and his nephew undertake a perilous journey deep into the center of the earth.

| | SF | 6–12 | |

Verne, Jules. *Twenty-Thousand Leagues Under the Sea.* Troll, 1990.

1372 This nineteenth century science fiction tale, entertains with the voyages, piracies, and disasters of a submarine ship. Students will enjoy comparing this story with present-day knowledge.

| | SF | 9–12 | |

Watson, Lyall. *The Water Planet.* Crown Publishers, 1988.

1373 Beautifully illustrated, this book discusses the physics and chemistry of water and describes its place in life science, physical science, and earth science.

| | NFN | 6–12 | P |

Weiner, Jonathan. *Planet Earth.* Bantam, 1986.

1374 The author covers all aspects of earth science. He describes water, land, air, and the environment. Beautiful photographs and diagrams accompany the text.

| | NFN | 9–12 | P |

Whitfield, Philip, and Joyce Pope. *Why Do the Seasons Change?* Viking, 1987.

1375 This book answers 113 wide-ranging questions often asked about nature.

| | NFI | 6–9 | I |

Wiesner, David. *Hurricane.* Houghton Mifflin, 1990.

1376 This bright picture book illustrates the strength of wind and tells how to prepare for a hurricane.

| | F | K–6 | I |

Wilcox, Charlotte. *Trash!* Lerner, 1989.

1377 This book examines the issue of solid waste management and discusses several methods of garbage disposal. Although most of the book deals with sanitary landfills, recycling is discussed as a way of reducing the amount of solid waste. [Ecology]

| | NFI | 3–9 | P |

Williams, Gene B. *Nuclear War, Nuclear Winter.* Franklin Watts, 1987.

1378 This thought-provoking book looks at the arms race, which has resulted in nuclear capability for many nations. The author discusses the catastrophic consequences of a nuclear war, such as the excessive heat and radiation that would destroy many organisms. [Ecology] [Technology]

| | NFI | 6–9 | I |

Williams, Terry. *Pieces of White Shell.* University of New Mexico, 1987.

1379 This novel combines ancient Navajo stories with modern scientific ideas. [Ecology]

| | NFN | 6–9 | |

Williams, Terry, and Ted Major. *The Secret Language of Snow.* Pantheon, 1984.

1380 The Kobuk Eskimos have ten different words for snow. Each chapter starts with one of these words and then discusses the meteorological conditions that produce the particular type of snow and the interactions of the animals with it.

| | NFN | 6–12 | I |

	Type of literature	Grade span	Illus- trations

Winckler, Suzanne, and Mary M. Rodgers. ***Our Endangered Planet: Population Growth.*** Lerner, 1991.
1381 The author discusses the effects of the increasing population of the world and the decreasing resources. [Ecology]

	NFI	3–9	P

Wright, Helen. ***Sweeper in the Sky: The Life of Maria Mitchell, First Woman Astronomer in America.*** Macmillan, 1949.
1382 This biography describes Maria Mitchell's enthusiasm, research, and dedication to astronomy. The social and political attitudes of her era are highlighted.

	B	9–12	

The subjects of the life sciences include the life processes of every living thing, from a microscopic cell to a magnificent blue whale or a mammoth redwood tree. Living things are described in many of the books cited, such as *Mammals and Their Milk,* by Lucia Anderson, *Redwoods Are the Tallest Trees in the World,* by David Adler, or *The Very Quiet Cricket,* by Eric Carle. Microscopic cells are described in books such as Paul De Kruif's *Microbe Hunters* or Greg Bear's science fiction book *Blood Music.* The history of genetics is the subject of *Genetics—From Mendel to Gene Splicing,* by Caroline Arnold. Ideas of evolution appear in many books, including Jonathan Miller's *Darwin for Beginners.* The connectedness of ecosystems is the subject of Patricia Lauber's *Sea Otters and Seaweed,* among others. *Cricket Songs: Japanese Haiku,* translated by Harry Behn, connects the natural world to poetry.

Life science processes are often explained in terms of the other sciences. Books such as Sylvia Johnson's *How Leaves Change* describe the chemistry of photosynthesis. Concepts of physics are illustrated in the way bats locate food, discussed in Johnson's *Bats.* The relationship among life sciences, geology, and climate is manifested in the way land regions define living communities, the subject of Thomas Wiewandt's *The Hidden Life of the Desert.*

	Type of literature	Grade span	Illus-trations
Adamson, Joy. ***Born Free: A Lioness of Two Worlds.*** Pantheon, 1987.	NFN	6–12	P
1383 This is a story about Elsa, the African lion raised by the author and her husband. They eventually realized that Elsa must also be trained to live in the wild. [Ecology]			
Adler, David A. ***Redwoods Are the Tallest Trees in the World.*** Crowell, 1978.	NFN	3–6	I
1384 A boy describes the surprise he felt when he first saw redwood trees. He also discusses their age and size and the environment they need. [Ecology]			
Adshead, Paul. ***A Peacock on the Roof.*** Child's Play, 1990.	NFN	K–3	I
1385 In this tale a peacock leaves home and places Man in an awkward predicament by reminding him of the dangers to both of their offspring.			
Aliki. ***Corn Is Maize: The Gift of the Indians.*** Harper, 1986.	NFN	K–3	I
1386 This book presents a comprehensive look at corn: its origins, history, planting, harvesting, and many uses.			
Aliki. ***A Weed Is a Flower: The Life of George Washington Carver.*** Simon and Schuster, 1988.	B	3–6	I
1387 This biography stresses George Washington Carver's love of learning and knowledge, in addition to his concern for people.			
Allison, Linda. ***Blood and Guts: A Working Guide to Your Own Insides.*** Little, Brown, 1976.	NFI	3–9	I
1388 The functions of the human body are introduced with facts, experiments, tests, and ideas for projects.			
Alpers, Antony. ***Dolphins: The Myth and the Mammal.*** Houghton Mifflin, 1961.	NFN	9–12	P
1389 Historical references, myths, legends, and true stories introduce dolphins. Also included is information about early research on their behaviors.			
Ancona, George. ***Turtle Watch.*** Macmillan, 1987.	NFN	3–6	P
1390 In this story, a seaside community is encouraged to save endangered sea turtles by finding their eggs, rescuing them, keeping them safe in a protected area, and returning the hatchlings to the sea. [Ecology]			

	Type of literature	Grade span	Illus-trations
Anderson, Lucia. *Mammals and Their Milk.* Putnam, 1984. **1391** The author presents much information about milk-producing mammals and about milk. Experiments and activities are also included in this book.	NFI	3–6	I
Anderson, Lucia. *The Smallest Life Around Us.* Crown Publishers, 1987. **1392** The microbes that are everywhere around us in our daily lives are illustrated and described in detail by the author.	NFI	3–9	I
Animal Migration and Navigation. Edited by S. A. Gathreaux, Jr. Academic, 1991. **1393** This book addresses animal migrations and explains these behaviors. The final chapter discusses current investigations of the earth's magnetic field as a possible explanation.	NFN	9–12	I
Animals, Animals. Edited by Laura Whipple. Putnam, 1989. **1394** This collection of animal-related poems is brightly illustrated; over 70 different animals are depicted.	P	K–6	I
Arnold, Caroline. *A Walk in the Desert.* Edited by Bonnie Brook. Silver Press, 1990. **1395** This beautifully illustrated volume introduces readers to the deserts of the world and to the plants and animals that frequently inhabit these locations. Also see the other books in this series, including *A Walk up the Mountain, A Walk by the Seashore,* and *A Walk in the Woods.* [Ecology]	NFN	K–6	I
Arnold, Caroline. *Cheetah.* William Morrow, 1989. **1396** The cheetah's place in the family of cats is discussed, as well as the environmental problems facing this species. [Ecology]	NFI	3–6	P
Arnold, Caroline. *Genetics: From Mendel to Gene Splicing.* Franklin Watts, 1986. **1397** This concise overview of genetics covers inherited diseases, genetic counseling, genetics in agriculture, and future applications of genetics.	NFI	6–12	
Arnold, Caroline. *Hippo.* William Morrow, 1989. **1398** Doodles, a baby hippopotamus at the San Francisco zoo, is the focus of this introduction to hippopotamuses and their environment.	NFI	3–6	P
Arnold, Caroline. *Kangaroo.* William Morrow, 1987. **1399** The story of the orphaned kangaroo Sport is used to discuss the history, habitat, physical characteristics, life-styles, and varieties of kangaroos.	NFI	3–6	P
Arnold, Caroline. *Llama.* William Morrow, 1988. **1400** The baby llama Gypsy is the focus of this book, which includes the history, importance, and value of llamas to the peoples of Central and South America.	NFI	3–6	P
Arnold, Caroline. *Penguin.* William Morrow, 1988. **1401** Photographs trace the life of two baby penguins at the San Francisco zoo. The author also discusses the natural habitats of penguins and compares the lives of wild penguins with those in zoos.	NFN	3–6	P
Arnold, Caroline. *Tule Elk.* Carolrhoda, 1989. **1402** This book provides detailed information about the California tule elk and describes the efforts of one person who helped save these endangered animals. [Ecology]	NFI	3–6	P

	Type of literature	Grade span	Illustrations
Arnold, Caroline. *A Walk on the Great Barrier Reef.* Carolrhoda, 1988. **1403** The many forms of life found on Australia's Great Barrier Reef are described in this book.	NFN	3–6	P
Arnosky, Jim. *Come Out, Muskrats.* William Morrow, 1991. **1404** A simple story and beautiful drawings tell of the muskrats' evening activities and habitat.	NFN	K–3	I
Arnosky, Jim. *Crinkleroot's Book of Animal Tracking.* Bradbury, 1989. **1405** Clever illustrations are used to identify the tracks of various animals and birds and to give information about their habits. [Ecology]	NFN	3–9	I
Arnosky, Jim. *In the Forest.* Lothrop, Lee and Shepard, 1989. **1406** The author shares his secrets for observing the variety of plants and animals who live in the forest. [Ecology]	NFN	3–9	I
Arnosky, Jim. *I Was Born in a Tree and Raised by Bees.* Bradbury, 1988. **1407** Old Crinkleroot cleverly demonstrates the skills of scientific observation, animal tracking, wilderness safety, and survival techniques through each season. [Ecology]	NFN	3–6	I
Arnosky, Jim. *A Kettle of Hawks.* Lothrop, Lee and Shepard, 1990. **1408** The author describes birds, animals, and insects that form groups, using color illustrations, short verses, and factual information.	P	3–9	I
Arnosky, Jim. *Secrets of a Wildlife Watcher.* Lothrop, Lee and Shepard, 1983. **1409** The author shares his techniques for finding, observing, and being sensitive to wild animals and birds. This book is good for the novice because it stresses the importance and value of recordkeeping. [Ecology]	NFN	6–9	I
Arthur, Alex. *Shell.* Knopf, 1989. **1410** The focus of this book is on creatures that have developed strong outer casings, or shells. The author discusses their camouflages, their places in the food chain, their histories, and the joys of collecting shells.	NFI	3–9	P
Asimov, Isaac. *Fantastic Voyage.* Bantam, 1988. **1411** This classic science fiction tale is about a group of four men and one woman who are miniaturized so that they can travel in a man's living body.	SF	9–12	
Attenborough, David. *The Living Planet: A Portrait of the Earth.* Little, Brown, 1986. **1412** Beautiful color photographs introduce and follow the evolution of life on earth. [Ecology]	NFI	6–12	P
Ayres, Pam. *When Dad Cuts Down the Chestnut Tree.* Knopf, 1988. **1413** In this story a young boy looks forward to all the things that he will be able to do when the chestnut tree is cut down. However, as he continues to think about the tree, he decides he wants to keep it. [Ecology]	NFN	3–6	I
Back, Christine. *Chicken and Egg.* Silver Burdett, 1989. **1414** A chick's development from a tiny spot on the egg yolk to a hatchling is explained and illustrated with color photographs.	NFI	K–3	P

	Type of literature	Grade span	Illus- trations
Back, Christine, and Barrie Watts. *Spider's Web.* Silver Burdett, 1986. **1415** This introduction to the common garden spider describes its orb web and shows how the web traps food.	NFI	K–6	P
Back, Christine, and Barrie Watts. *Tadpole and Frog.* Silver Burdett, 1986. **1416** The life cycle of frogs and their place in the food chain are explained in this simple book.	NFI	K–6	P
Baker, Jeannie. *Where the Forest Meets the Sea.* Greenwillow, 1988. **1417** Collage illustrations enhance the story of a young boy's day trip to the Australian rain forest.	F	3–6	I
Baker, Olaf. *Where the Buffaloes Begin.* Viking, 1989. **1418** A Native American boy experiences the beauty, power, and natural wonders of the prairie while searching for the lake where the buffaloes began. [Ecology]	NFN	6–9	I
Bare, Colleen Stanley. *Never Kiss an Alligator.* Dutton, 1989. **1419** This clever book stresses that alligators are dangerous wild reptiles that must be respected and also protected.	NFI	K–3	P
Bash, Barbara. *Desert Giant: The World of the Saguaro Cactus.* Little, Brown, 1989. **1420** Delicate watercolors and an interesting text describe the birds, insects, and reptiles whose homes are found in both living and dead saguaro cactus.	NFN	3–6	I
Bash, Barbara. *Tree of Life: The World of the African Baobab.* Little, Brown, 1989. **1421** The importance of the African baobab tree to the animal kingdom is described in this colorful book.	NFN	3–6	I
Bash, Barbara. *Urban Roosts: Where Birds Nest in the City.* Little, Brown, 1990. **1422** This book explains how different varieties of birds have adapted to life in cities.	NFN	3–6	I
Baylor, Byrd. *The Desert Is Theirs.* Aladdin, 1987. **1423** This poem, an integration of myth and fact, explains why some people and animals love living in the desert. [Ecology]	P	K–6	I
Baylor, Byrd. *Desert Voices.* Scribner Books for Young Readers, 1981. **1424** These poems are about the different animals that live in the desert. In each poem a different creature describes its life and its place in the desert's ecosystem.	F	3–9	I
Baylor, Byrd. *Guess Who My Favorite Person Is?* Scribner Books for Young Readers, 1992. **1425** In this poem a guessing game involves selecting and describing favorite things. The descriptions emphasize both observational skills and clarity of thought.	F	K–3	I
Baylor, Byrd. *Hawk, I'm Your Brother.* Aladdin, 1986. **1426** This poem tells the story of a Native American boy who attempts to tame a fledgling hawk. The boy finally realizes that a wild hawk must be free. [Ecology]	F	K–6	I

	Type of literature	Grade span	Illus-trations

Bear, Greg. *Blood Music.* Ace, 1986. — SF — 9–12

1427 This science fiction tale is about the creation of intelligent microorganisms that cause a worldwide epidemic.

Bellamy, David. *The Mouse Book.* Oriel, 1983. — F — 6–9 — S

1428 This engaging story, told from the perspective of a mouse, traces the natural history of mice.

Bellamy, David. *Our Changing World: The Rock Pool.* Crown Publishers, 1988. — NFI — K–6 — S

1429 Colorful scientific drawings illustrate the variety of creatures and plants that live above and below the waterline of an oceanic rock pool. In the story a ship leaks oil that kills most life in the pool. The cleanup and the return of life are carefully described. [Ecology] Also see other titles in the *Our Changing World* series: *The Forest, The River, the Roadside.*

Berger, Melvin. *Why I Cough, Sneeze, Shiver, Hiccup and Yawn.* Harper, 1983. — NFI — K–3 — I

1430 This book is a simple introduction to basic reflexes of the body.

Bjork, Christina. *Elliot's Extraordinary Cookbook.* Farrar, Straus and Giroux, 1991. — F — 6–9 — I

1431 This delightful book explains basic nutrition and the digestive process. Some tasty recipes are included.

Bjork, Christina. *Linnea's Almanac.* Farrar, Straus and Giroux, 1989. — NFN — K–6 — I

1432 A city girl introduces general scientific facts involving seeds, plants, and birds in a delightful, engaging way.

Bjork, Christina. *Linnea's Windowsill Garden.* Farrar, Straus and Giroux, 1988. — NFN — K–6 — I

1433 A city girl explains the variety of her projects and activities with birds, seeds, and plants. [Ecology]

Bodanis, David. *The Secret House.* Simon and Schuster, 1986. — NFN — 9–12 — P

1434 An invisible world that inhabits our homes is presented with photomicrographs. [Ecology]

Bonners, Susan. *A Penguin Year.* Delacorte, 1981. — NFN — K–3 — I

1435 The Adélie penguin of the South Pole is the subject of this book. Special emphasis is given the care they give their young.

Bourne, Geoffrey H. *Primate Odyssey.* Putnam, 1974. — NFN — 9–12

1436 Great apes are the primary subjects of the research projects described.

Brady, Irene. *Elephants on the Beach.** Scribner's, 1979. — NFN — 3–6 — P

1437 The author provides a narrative description of her observations of elephant seals. This book illustrates careful observation as a scientific process.

Branley, Franklyn M. *Shivers and Goose Bumps: How We Keep Warm.* Harper, 1984. — NFI — 3–9 — I

1438 Body warmth is defined, and the different ways creatures retain body heat are described. Also included are methods for heating homes and for keeping space travelers warm.

	Type of literature	Grade span	Illustrations
Brenner, Barbara. *A Snake-Lover's Diary.* Harper, 1990. **1439** This handbook covers basic information on snakes, including their capture, care, feeding, and return to the wild.	NFN	3–6	P
Brenner, Barbara, and May Garelick. *Two Orphan Cubs.* Walker and Company, 1989. **1440** A wildlife scientist tells about rescuing two newborn bear cubs and finding them a foster mother.	NFN	K–3	I
Brett, Jan. *The First Dog.* Harcourt Brace Jovanovich, 1988. **1441** A cave boy realizes that a hungry wolf could be a helpful friend in this story. The pictures and setting were inspired by cave paintings from the Pleistocene period.	F	3–6	I
Brooks, Bruce. *On the Wing: The Life of Birds from Feathers to Flight.* Scribner's, 1989. **1442** These essays about the lives of birds are beautifully written and accompanied by magnificent photographs.	NFN	6–12	P
Brothwell, Don. *The Bog Man and the Archaeology of People.* Harvard, 1987. **1443** The scientific tests performed on bog bodies are explained. These tests provide information about early humans' diseases, foods, cultural practices, causes of death, and environment.	NFI	9–12	P
Brown, Pam. *Florence Nightingale: The Founder of Modern Nursing.* Adapted by Mary Nolan. Stevens, 1991. **1444** This biography describes Florence Nightingale's personal life, her contributions establishing nursing as a profession, and her efforts revolutionizing the medical care of the sick.	B	3–9	
Bunting, Eve. *The Sea World Book of Sharks.* Harcourt Brace Jovanovich, 1984. **1445** This comprehensive introduction to sharks has many unusual color photographs of the different species of sharks.	NFI	3–9	P
Burleigh, Robert. *A Man Named Thoreau.* Atheneum, 1985. **1446** This is a simple introduction to Henry Thoreau's philosophy of life, his writings, and his love of nature.	B	3–9	I
Burnie, David. *Plant.* Knopf, 1989. **1447** The author provides simple definitions of plants and then moves on to complex concepts. The color photographs enhance the text and clarify the concepts. This volume is part of the EYEWITNESS BOOKS series. [Ecology]	NFI	3–9	P
Burnie, David. *Tree.* Knopf, 1988. **1448** Trees are defined by their evolutionary types in this book, which also includes information on the uses of woods, the care and management of trees as resources, and ways to study trees. The crisp photographs enhance the text. This is a part of the EYEWITNESS BOOKS series. [Ecology]	NFI	3–9	P
Burton, Robert. *Eggs: Nature's Perfect Package.* Facts on File, 1987. **1449** Wonderful color photographs provide an in-depth look at the incredible variety of strategies animals use to produce, fertilize, and care for their eggs.	NFI	6–12	P

	Type of literature	Grade span	Illustrations
Burton, Virginia. *Life Story.* Houghton Mifflin, 1989. **1450** The history of the earth and the evolution of its flora and fauna are presented as a colorful stage play.	NFN	K–6	I
Bushey, Jerry. *Farming the Land: Modern Farmers and Their Machines.* Carolrhoda, 1987. **1451** The machinery that makes modern farming possible is introduced with pictures showing plowing, tilling, disking, fertilizing, mowing, and harvesting. [Technology]	NFI	6–9	P
Caras, Roger. *A Cat Is Watching: A Look at the Way Cats See Us.* Simon and Schuster, 1989. **1452** Domestic cats are introduced through anecdotes.	NFI	9–12	
Carle, Eric. *The Honeybee and the Robber: A Moving Picture Book.* Putnam, 1981. **1453** This simple story follows the course of bees from flower to flower. Also included is a page of facts about bees.	F	K–3	I
Carle, Eric. *The Tiny Seed.* Picture Book Studio, 1990. **1454** Seeds that are blown about have adventures before landing on suitable soil and growing into plants. Dramatic illustrations accompany the text.	F	K–3	I
Carle, Eric. *The Very Quiet Cricket.* Putnam, 1990. **1455** A voiceless cricket meets a variety of lovely insects. As he tries one last time to say hello, the turn of a page produces a "chirp."	F	K–3	I
Carrick, Carol. *In the Moonlight.* Clarion Books, 1990. **1456** A family shares the excitement of spring lambing and the joy of seeing a newborn lamb.	P	3–6	I
Carrighar, Sally. *One Day at Teton Marsh.* University of Nebraska, 1979. **1457** In this collection of short stories, readers have the sense of entering the world of anthropomorphic animals. [Ecology]	F	9–12	I
Carrighar, Sally. *One Day on Beetle Rock.* University of Nebraska, 1978. **1458** This collection of short stories anthropomorphizes a variety of life forms found in the wild and gives the reader the feeling of entering each animal's world. [Ecology]	F	9–12	I
Cherry, Lynne. *The Great Kapok Tree: A Tale of the Amazon Rain Forest.* Harcourt Brace Jovanovich, 1990. **1459** As a man naps under a kapok tree in the rain forest, he dreams about all of the beautiful creatures that depend on this tree. Each creature sadly tells what will happen to it if the tree is cut down. The man awakens, throws down his axe, and leaves the rain forest. [Ecology]	F	K–6	I
Clarke, Barry. *Amazing Frogs and Toads.* Knopf, 1991. **1460** Crisp color photographs introduce a variety of frogs and toads. See the other books in this JUNIOR EYEWITNESS series.	NFI	3–6	P
Cleaver, Vera, and Bill Cleaver. *Where the Lilies Bloom.* Harper, 1969. **1461** In this story Appalachian children survive after their father's death by harvesting and selling wild herbs, roots, and plants.	F	6–9	

	Type of literature	Grade span	Illus-trations
Climo, Shirley. *Someone Saw a Spider: Spider Facts and Folktales.* Harper, 1985. **1462** Spider legends, myths, and folktales are taken from many cultures around the world. A fascinating Greek myth starts this collection, and an equally fascinating true story from Louisiana closes it. This would be a delightful book to read aloud. [Folklore]	NFN	3–9	I
Coats, Laura Jane. *The Oak Tree.** Macmillan, 1987. **1463** This is a simple story that introduces the creatures who use an old oak tree during a 24-hour period. [Ecology]	F	K–3	I
Colbert, Edwin H., and Michael Morales. *Evolution of the Vertebrates.* John Wiley, n.d. **1464** The author traces the evolution of backboned animals as revealed in fossil remains.	NFN	9–12	I
Coldrey, Jennifer. *Strawberry.* Silver Burdett, 1989. **1465** Photographs illustrate the stages of a strawberry plant's development, the fruit itself, and the start of new plants.	NFI	3–6	P
Cole, Joanna. *Evolution: The Story of How Life Developed on Earth.* Harper, 1989. **1466** This introductory book explains the order of the fossil layers and the evolution of the lobe-fin fish into amphibians, the ancestors of reptiles.	NFN	3–6	I
Cole, Joanna. *How You Were Born.* William Morrow, 1985. **1467** This is a warm, loving description of human conception, gestation, birth, and infancy. Photographs enhance the sense of joy and happiness the family experiences with the new baby. This is a good book to share with a young child.	NFI	3–6	P
Cole, Joanna. *The Human Body: How We Evolved.* William Morrow, 1987. **1468** This is an introduction to the history, development, and evolution of the human form, with comparisons to other creatures. Significantly, the author points out that while the human form has not changed in 10,000 years, cultures are constantly changing.	NFN	3–9	I
Cole, Joanna. *Large as Life Animals in Beautiful Life-Size Paintings.* Knopf, 1990. **1469** Life-size pictures of small diurnal and nocturnal animals accompany brief text describing each creature. The color illustrations are exquisitely detailed.	NFI	K–6	I
Cole, Joanna. *The Magic School Bus: Inside the Human Body.* Scholastic, 1990. **1470** This fantasy field trip inside a student's body takes the class for on-site visits to the major internal organs. Humor makes learning about the circulatory system, the brain, the nervous system, and muscles enjoyable.	NFN	K–6	I
Cole, Joanna. *My Puppy Is Born.* William Morrow, 1991. **1471** A girl describes awaiting the birth of a puppy and then watching it grow up enough to leave its mother and go home with her.	NFI	3–6	P

	Type of literature	Grade span	Illus-trations
Cole, Joanna. *A Snake's Body.* William Morrow, 1981. **1472** This book introduces snakes, including their anatomy, methods of movement, hunting and eating techniques, and the hatching of their eggs.	NFI	3–6	P
Connor, Judith. *Kelp Forests.* Monterey Bay Aquarium, 1989. **1473** The habitats, interactions, and communities found in a Monterey Bay kelp forest are pictured and discussed in this book.	NFI	9–12	P
Cousteau, Jacques. *The Silent World.* Isis, 1989. **1474** Cousteau describes what it is like to swim with sea creatures, explore sunken ships, and recover lost artifacts. [Ecology]	NFN	9–12	P
Cousteau, Jacques, and James Dugan. *The Living Sea.* Lyons and Burford, 1988. **1475** This classic introduces the underwater world and the strange creatures and plants who inhabit that world. [Ecology]	NFN	9–12	P
Cousteau, Jacques-Yves. *The Whale: Mighty Monarch of the Sea.* Doubleday, 1972. **1476** This is a fascinating account of Cousteau's experiences with many different types of whales. [Ecology]	NFN	6–12	P
Cowcher, Helen. *Antarctica.* Farrar, Straus and Giroux, 1990. **1477** In this beautifully illustrated and unique book Adélie penguins hatch their eggs, survive, and then are frightened by humans' intrusion. [Ecology]	NFN	K–6	I
Cowcher, Helen. *Rain Forest.* Farrar, Straus and Giroux, 1990. **1478** Marvelous illustrations enhance descriptions of the fear of animals as their rain forest is being cut down. [Ecology]	F	K–3	I
Crichton, Michael. *Jurassic Park.* Knopf, 1990. **1479** The ethics of DNA cloning are explored in this scientific thriller, in which a DNA is developed to create live dinosaurs for the ultimate theme park. As the novel progresses, the dinosaurs and the master plan run amok.	SF	9–12	
Cricket Songs: Japanese Haiku. Translated by Harry Behn. Harcourt Brace and World, 1964. **1480** Japanese haiku evokes many beautiful images of natural wonders.	P	3–9	I
Cristini, Ermanno, and Luigi Puricelli. *In the Woods.* Picture Book Studio, 1985. **1481** The author's illustrations introduce the animals and plants that inhabit a forest in this colorful, wordless picture book. There are identification pages for all of the wildlife shown. This book is one in a series that also includes *In the Pond* and *In My Garden.* [Ecology]	NFI	K–3	I
Curtis, Neil. *Discovering Snakes and Lizards.* Watts, 1986. **1482** The author discusses the evolution, physical characteristics, and habitats of reptiles. The photographs create a desire to learn more about reptiles.	NFI	6–9	I
Dabcovich, Lydia. *Busy Beavers.* Dutton, 1988. **1483** Colorful illustrations highlight the activities of a beaver family.	F	K–3	I
Dabcovich, Lydia. *Sleepy Bear.* Dutton, 1982. **1484** This is a simple story about a wild bear that sleeps through the winter in his cozy cave until spring returns.	F	K–3	I

	Type of literature	Grade span	Illus- trations
Dallinger, Jane, and Cynthia Overbeck. *Swallowtail Butterflies.* Lerner, 1982.	NFI	K–3	P
1485 Swallowtail butterflies are introduced in this book that covers their physical characteristics, life cycle, and ecosystem.			
Dallinger, Jane, and Sylvia A. Johnson. *Frogs and Toads.* Lerner, 1982.	NFI	K–3	P
1486 The author points out the differences and similarities between frogs and toads and describes their physical characteristics, their metamorphosis, and their importance in the food chain.			
De Kruif, Paul. *Microbe Hunters.* Harcourt Brace Jovanovich, 1966.	NFN	6–12	
1487 These dramatic stories highlight the curiosity and enthusiasm of scientists who have discovered new worlds under their microscopes.			
Desowitz, Robert S. *The Thorn in the Starfish: The Human Immune System and How It Works.* Norton, 1988.	NFI	9–12	
1488 This is an easy-to-read discussion of classic and current studies in immunology. The author demonstrates the scientific method being used in real-life situations. Some educators consider this book essential for high school students.			
Dewey, Jennifer O. *Animal Architecture.* Orchard Books, 1991.	NFI	6–9	I
1489 With extraordinary details a variety of animals' homes are described and illustrated.			
Dewey, Jennifer O. *A Night and Day in the Desert.* Little, Brown, 1991.	NFN	K–6	I
1490 This beautifully illustrated book about the desert describes how plants and animals have adapted to survive in a harsh environment.			
Diagram Group. *The Brain: A User's Manual.* Putnam, 1987.	NFI	6–12	I
1491 Clear, concise descriptions cover every aspect of the brain's anatomy and physiology.			
Dickinson, Peter. *Eva.* Dell, 1990.	SF	6–12	
1492 In this futuristic novel Eva's brain is transferred into a chimp's body during experimental surgery. While medical technology saves Eva's life, she must adjust to being trapped in the wrong body.			
Dillard, Annie. *Pilgrim at Tinker Creek.* Harper, 1988.	NFN	9–12	
1493 The author vividly describes the birds and animals that inhabit the world around her.			
Dorros, Arthur. *Ant Cities.* Harper, 1988.	NFN	3–6	I
1494 The author describes the colonies and specialized tasks of ants. Instructions are also included for building an ant farm.			
Doubilet, Anne. *Under the Sea from A to Z.* Crown Publishers, 1991.	NFI	3–9	P
1495 This alphabet book has color photographs and descriptions of unusual sea creatures and plants.			
Douglas-Hamilton, Iain, and Oria Douglas-Hamilton. *Among the Elephants.* Viking, 1975.	NFN	9–12	P
1496 In this personal description of their life among the elephants, the authors come to regard them with awe and affection. The last chapter discusses the severity of the crisis facing elephants and their need for protection.			

	Type of literature	Grade span	Illustrations
Dow, Lesley. *Alligators and Crocodiles.* Facts on File, 1990. **1497** This definitive look at alligators and crocodiles covers their history, habitat, physical characteristics, hunting methods, care of their young, and methods of survival. Color photographs accompany the text.	NFI	6–12	P
Dowden, Anne Ophelia. *The Clover and the Bee: A Book of Pollination.* Harper, 1990. **1498** Pollination and the delicate relationship between plants and insects are explained in this book. Colorful scientific drawings accompany the text.	NFI	3–9	S
Dowie, Mark. *We Have a Donor: The Bold New World of Organ Transplants.* St. Martin's, 1988. **1499** Organ transplantation for the critically ill is debated as the author discusses one donor's "gift" of his body's organs. [Technology]	NFN	9–12	
Downer, John. *Supersense: Perceptions in the Natural World.* Henry Holt, 1989. **1500** The author discusses the senses used by animals. Color photographs accompany the text.	NFI	9–12	P
Dr. Seuss. *The Lorax.* Random House, 1971. **1501** In this tale about exploitation of the environment, "truffula trees" are used to make "thneeds," causing the forest to be reduced to nothing. [Ecology]	F	K–6	I
Durrell, Gerald. *Keeper.* Arcade, 1991. **1502** Keeper, a boxer dog, visits his animal friends every morning and learns about the zoo animals.	F	3–6	I
Eckert, Allan W. *Incident at Hawk's Hill.* Little, Brown, 1971. **1503** This Canadian survival story is based on a true incident. A female badger adopts Ben and helps him have an incredible summer in the wilderness. [Ecology]	F	6–9	
Ehlert, Lois. *Planting a Rainbow.* Harcourt Brace Jovanovich, 1988. **1504** The proper planting of seeds and bulbs is illustrated in this book. The resulting flowers form a bright rainbow of colors.	F	K–3	I
Eiseley, Loren. *All the Strange Hours: The Excavation of a Life.* *Macmillan, 1977. **1505** This autobiography of the noted naturalist covers his childhood, graduate school experiences, and descriptions of his field studies. The last chapter reveals his personal philosophy in a symbolic way.	NFN	9–12	
Eldredge, Niles. *Lifepulse: Episodes from the Story of the Fossil Record.* Facts on File, 1987. **1506** This naturalist shares his love of paleontology, fossils, and history. He includes day-by-day scientific work and a peek through a little window into a world of 55 million years ago.	NFN	9–12	I
Engdahl, Sylvia L. *Enchantress from the Stars.* Peter Smith, 1991. **1507** In this science fiction tale about saving the planet Andrecia, Elana becomes both an enchantress and a legend.	SF	6–9	

	Type of literature	Grade span	Illus-trations

Esbensen, Barbara Juster. *Great Northern Diver: The Loon.* Little, Brown, 1990.
> **1508** The elusive, primitive loon is introduced in this book that has detailed color illustrations showing their unusual markings. The text describes their unusual markings, their migratory patterns, their habitat, and the raising of their young.

	NFN	3–6	I

Esbensen, Barbara Juster. *The Star Maiden: An Ojibway Tale.* Little, Brown, 1988.
> **1509** Exquisite illustrations enhance this Native American myth about a star that wishes to live on earth and becomes a water lily.

	NFN	3–6	I

Facklam, Margery. *And Then There Was One: The Mysteries of Extinction.* Sierra Club Books, 1990.
> **1510** George, the last saddle-back tortoise, is the focus of these discussions on evolution, extinction, and current conservation efforts.

	NFN	3–9	I

Facklam, Margery. *Do Not Disturb: The Mysteries of Animal Hibernation and Sleep.* Little, Brown, 1989.
> **1511** Current research is introduced on hibernation, deep sleep, light sleep, cold-blooded sleepers, the daily dormants, and the state of animals during sleep.

	NFN	3–9	I

Facklam, Margery. *Partners for Life: The Mysteries of Animal Symbiosis.* Sierra Club Books, 1989.
> **1512** The benefits of partnerships among animals for providing food, shelter, comfort, or protection is the subject of this book.

	NFI	3–9	I

Facklam, Margery, and Howard Facklam. *Spare Parts for People.* Harcourt Brace Jovanovich, 1987.
> **1513** This fascinating book includes both human interest stories and the prerequisite biology for understanding the development of such parts as mechanical hearts, designer bones, and computer-assisted walking systems that currently can enhance or prolong lives.

	NFI	6–12	P

Featherly, Jay. *Ko-hoh: The Call of the Trumpeter Swan.* Carolrhoda, 1986.
> **1514** An introduction to North America's only native swan includes wonderful photographs of adult swans as well as their nests, eggs, and cygnets.

	NFI	3–9	P

Featherly, Jay. *Mustangs: Wild Horses of the American West.* Carolrhoda, 1986.
> **1515** This history of horses in North America includes information about their ability to survive as wild horses and their effects on the environment. [Ecology]

	NFI	3–9	P

Ferguson, Ava. *Sharks and Rays of the Pacific Coast.* Monterey Bay Aquarium, 1990.
> **1516** Many of the 33 kinds of sharks and their relatives found in the Monterey Bay region are pictured and described in this book.

	NFI	6–9	P

	Type of literature	Grade span	Illus-trations
Fine, Judylaine. *Afraid to Ask: A Book for Families to Share About Cancer.* William Morrow, 1991. **1517** This is a straightforward book that defines and explains the types of cancer describes their treatments, and suggests strategies for living with a cancer diagnosis.	NFI	6–12	
Fischer-Nagel, Heiderose, and Andreas Fischer-Nagel. *An Ant Colony.* Carolrhoda Books, 1985. **1518** Wonderful enlarged color photographs and a scientific text provide in-depth information about ants, including their life cycles, varieties, colonies, and community life.	NFI	3–6	P
Fischer-Nagel, Heiderose, and Andreas Fischer-Nagel. *The Housefly.* Carolrhoda, 1990. **1519** Colorful, close-up photographs of the common housefly and a comprehensive text provide in-depth information about its life cycle, anatomy, and value to ecology.	NFI	3–6	P
Fischer-Nagel, Heiderose, and Andreas Fischer-Nagel. *Inside the Burrow: The Life of the Golden Hamster.* Carolrhoda, 1986. **1520** Colorful photographs allow observation of a mother hamster's burrow and the growth and development of her babies. The authors include information about the history of hamsters, their life cycles, and proper care of pet hamsters.	NFI	3–6	P
Fischer-Nagel, Heiderose, and Andreas Fischer-Nagel. *Life of the Butterfly.* Carolrhoda, 1987. **1521** Fantastic photographs and a scientific text introduce the butterfly's life cycle, physical characteristics, and varieties. This book is one of a series that also includes such books as *The Life of a Ladybug* and *The Life of a Honeybee.*	NFI	3–6	P
Fischer-Nagel, Heiderose, and Andreas Fischer-Nagel. *A Look Through the Mouse Hole.* Carolrhoda, 1989. **1522** Exquisite color photographs follow the adventures of a couple of house mice as they establish a new home and raise their family in the authors' basement. Abundant information is provided about house mice in general, their differences compared to other mice and moles, and the care and feeding of pet mice.	NFI	3–6	P
Fischer-Nagel, Heiderose, and Andreas Fischer-Nagel. *Season of the White Stork.* Carolrhoda Books, 1984. **1523** The European white stork is introduced with specific information about its migratory habits, life cycle, young, and current international efforts to protect this unique bird.	NFI	3–6	P
Fleischman, Paul. *Joyful Noise: Poems for Two Voices.* Harper, 1988. **1524** From grasshoppers to whirligig beetles, the insect world comes alive in the musical language of these 14 poems.	P	3–9	I
Fleischman, Paul. *Path of the Pale Horse.* Harper, 1983. **1525** This novel, set in Philadelphia in 1793, tells the story of the yellow fever epidemic as seen by a boy who is a doctor's apprentice.	F	6–9	

	Type of literature	Grade span	Illus-trations

Flora. *Feathers Like a Rainbow: An Amazon Indian Tale.* Harper, 1989.

1526 Bright illustrations help tell of a baby bird's wish for beautiful colored feathers, his mother's efforts to grant his wish, and the colors that were left for him after the other birds stole most of the colors.

	NFN	3–6	I

Florian, Douglas. *A Turtle Day.* Harper, 1989.

1527 This simple story is about a turtle's daily activities.

	NFN	K–3	I

Forsyth, Adrian. *The Architecture of Animals.* Firefly, 1989.

1528 The construction methods and materials employed by animals in building their homes and the impact these structures have on the environment are explored in this book.

	NFI	6–9	P

Forsyth, Adrian. *Journey Through a Tropical Jungle.* Simon and Schuster, 1989.

1529 Marvelous photographs enhance descriptions of the inhabitants of Costa Rica's rain forest. This biologist also discusses the valuable contributions rain forests make to the quality of our lives and the current worldwide imbalance of resources and wealth.

	NFN	3–9	P

Fossey, Diane. *Gorillas in the Mist.* Houghton Mifflin, 1988.

1530 Diane Fossey writes about her work with four family groups of mountain gorillas. She describes her research, her victories, and her frustrations with both the working conditions and the poachers who slaughter gorillas. [Ecology]

	NFN	9–12	P

Frank, Julia. *Alzheimer's Disease: The Silent Epidemic.* Lerner, 1985.

1531 Several case studies personalize the information presented on Alzheimer's disease, including its causes, current research, possible cures, and the pattern this disease follows.

	NFI	6–12	

Freedman, Russell. *Rattlesnakes.* Holiday House, 1984.

1532 Rattlesnakes' habitat, behaviors, varieties, physical characteristics, and life cycles are described in this book that includes many photographs.

	NFI	3–9	P

Freedman, Russell. *Sharks.* Holiday House, 1985.

1533 The author takes a global look at sharks, pointing out their similarities and differences, physical characteristics, hunting styles, eating habits, and usefulness to humans. This book has many color photographs.

	NFI	3–6	P

Gallant, Roy A. *Before the Sun Dies: The Story of Evolution.* Macmillan, 1989.

1534 Current scientific theory is presented on the development of the solar system, our planet, and the primitive life forms that adapted to changes.

	NFI	6–12	P

Gardner, Martin. *Science: Good, Bad and Bogus.* Prometheus, 1981.

1535 This collection of essays investigates the fakery and fraud that sometimes masquerade as science.

	NFN	9–12	

George, Jean Craighead. *The Grizzly Bear with the Golden Ears.* Harper, 1982.

1536 A brown grizzly bear in Alaska learns to steal food, with unfortunate consequences.

	F	3–6	I

	Type of literature	Grade span	Illus-trations
George, Jean Craighead. *Julie of the Wolves.* Harper, 1972. **1537** Julie describes her travels across Alaska, the problems of survival, and her acceptance by a wolf pack before she finally reaches her father. [Ecology]	F	6–9	
George, Jean Craighead. *My Side of the Mountain.* Dutton, 1988. **1538** In this survival story Sam runs from city life to the mountains where he quickly learns to make shelters, build fires, catch fish, and make friends with the animals. However, he soon realizes his need for human companionship.	F	6–9	
George, Jean Craighead. *One Day in the Tropical Rain Forest.* Harper, 1990. **1539** The ecology of the tropical rain forest is explored in this novel about a young boy and a scientist who seek a butterfly as bulldozers are waiting to begin clearing the land. [Ecology]	NFN	3–6	I
George, Jean Craighead. *The Talking Earth.* Harper, 1987. **1540** In this story a young Seminole Indian girl ventures into the Florida Everglades alone. She tests her ancestors' legends and learns the importance of listening to the earth's messages. [Ecology]	F	6–9	
George, Jean Craighead. *Water Sky.* Harper, 1989. **1541** This novel is about a boy in Alaska who searches for his uncle. The importance of whaling to the Eskimo people is vividly portrayed when the boy spends time at the whaling camp at Barrow.	L	6–9	
George, Jean Craighead. *The Wounded Wolf.* Harper, 1978. **1542** The black-and-white drawings in this novel help to convey a wounded wolf's desperate plight as it is stalked by predators.	F	3–6	I
George, William T. *Beaver at Long Pond.* Greenwillow, 1988. **1543** Full-color illustrations help tell about a beaver's adventures, habitat, and methods to repair its dam. [Ecology]	NFI	K–3	I
George, William T. *Box Turtle at Long Pond.* Greenwillow, 1989. **1544** Beautiful, meticulous illustrations combine with the text to introduce a box turtle's habitat and daily activities. [Ecology]	NFI	K–3	I
Gibbons, Gail. *From Seed to Plant.* Holiday House, 1991. **1545** Beautiful illustrations follow the development of seeds from flowers. The text describes both the pollination and germination of plants.	NFI	K–3	I
Gibbons, Gail. *The Milk Makers.* Macmillan Children's Book Group, 1987. **1546** Cows are introduced as our primary source of milk. This book describes methods of caring for cows and the processes of milking them, both manual and automated.	NFI	K–3	I
Gibbons, Gail. *Monarch Butterfly.* Holiday House, 1989. **1547** The monarch butterfly's life cycle, migration patterns, and physical characteristics are introduced. Information is also included for the care of a captive caterpillar and chrysalis and about the releasing of a newly hatched butterfly.	NFI	K–6	I
Gibbons, Gail. *Prehistoric Animals.* Holiday House, 1988. **1548** This is a simple introduction to a variety of giant prehistoric animals.	NFI	K–3	I

	Type of literature	Grade span	Illustrations

Gibbons, Gail. *Zoo.* Harper, 1991. — NFI / K–3 / I

1549 The daily behind-the-scenes work at a zoo is introduced, such as feeding the animals and cleaning their cages, caring for sick animals, building new exhibits, and preparing for the visiting public.

Gohier, Francois. *A Pod of Gray Whales.* Blake, 1987. — NFI / 6–9 / P

1550 The California gray whale's life is described in the book. The text is enhanced with excellent photographs. [Ecology]

Goldberg, Jeff. *Anatomy of a Scientific Discovery.* Bantam, 1988. — NFN / 9–12

1551 The discovery of endorphins began with the theory that naturally occurring morphine is produced in animals' bodies. This book highlights the race for this profitable drug, illuminates topics in modern biochemistry, and gives a behind-the-scenes peek into the scientific community.

Goodall, Jane. *The Chimpanzee Family Book.* Picture Book Studio, 1989. — NFI / 3–6 / P

1552 Chimpanzees' family relationships are introduced in this picture book that has charming pictures.

Goodall, Jane. *In the Shadow of Man.* Houghton Mifflin, 1983. — NFN / 9–12 / P

1553 Jane Goodall describes her studies of the behaviors and social structures of chimpanzees. [Ecology]

Goor, Ron, and Nancy Goor. *Insect Metamorphosis: From Egg to Adult.* Atheneum, 1990. — NFI / K–6 / P

1554 Superb color photographs and text introduce both complete and incomplete metamorphosis with a variety of intriguing examples.

Gordon, Bernard L. *The Secret Life of Fishes.* Book and Tackle, 1980. — NFI / 9–12 / I

1555 In this book both freshwater and saltwater fish are described, both of which have some eccentric quality or behavior that makes them fascinating.

Gorman, James. *The Man with No Endorphins and Other Reflections on Science.* Viking, 1989. — NFN / 9–12

1556 These short, humorous essays are suitable for reading aloud.

Gould, James, and Carol Gould. *Sexual Selections.* Freeman, 1989. — NFN / 9–12

1557 Examples of courtship rituals and mating behaviors are explored and woven into theories that explain how these behaviors ensure continuity of species.

Gould, Stephen Jay. *Ever Since Darwin: Reflections in Natural History.* Norton, 1979. — NFN / 9–12

1558 These essays focus on proposals for modifications of Darwin's theory.

Gould, Stephen Jay. *The Flamingo's Smile: Reflections in Natural History.* Norton, 1987. — NFI / 9–12

1559 Gould continues his practice of exploring evolution from every angle—historical, philosophical, and scholastic. This is lively reading.

Gould, Stephen Jay. *Hen's Teeth and Horse's Toes.* Norton, 1984. — NFN / 9–12

1560 This collection of essays deals with both the scientific and the political issues of evolution.

	Type of literature	Grade span	Illus- trations
Gross, Ruth Belov. *A Book About Your Skeleton.* Scholastic, 1978. **1561** The bones in our bodies are discussed in this book, including why we need them, how they are connected, how they are used, and how to keep them healthy.	NFI	K–6	I
Gross, Ruth Belov. *What Do Animals Eat?** Four Winds Press, 1971. **1562** This book examines and discusses the diets of a variety of animals, from porcupines to people. It also looks at how these animals obtain their food and how they digest it.	NFI	K–3	I
Hall, Howard. *Sharks: The Perfect Predators.* Blake, 1990. **1563** This book includes pictures of sharks in action in their natural habitats.	NFI	6–9	P
Halton, Cheryl Mays. *Those Amazing Leeches.** Macmillan, 1989. **1564** This book covers the history, importance to medical research, physical characteristics, life cycles, and natural habitats of leeches. It also explains how they are raised for commercial purposes.	NFI	6–9	P
Heinrich, Bernd. *In a Patch of Fireweed.* Harvard, 1984. **1565** Field biologists are a very special group of scientists whose attention to detail and minutiae sets them apart. This German naturalist describes in very picturesque fashion his observations of nature's creatures.	B	9–12	
Heinrich, Bernd. *One Man's Owl.* Princeton, 1987. **1566** A great horned owlet that was too young to survive alone becomes part of a human family. [Ecology]	NFN	9–12	I
Heller, Ruth. *Animals Born Alive and Well.* Putnam, 1982. **1567** This lyrical book with intriguing illustrations tells how animals are classified according to how they are born.	NFN	K–6	I
Heller, Ruth. *Chickens Aren't the Only Ones.* Putnam, 1981. **1568** This beautifully illustrated book shows the creatures other than chickens that also lay eggs. Also see Ruth Heller's book *Animals Born Alive and Well.*	NFN	K–3	I
Heller, Ruth. *How to Hide a Polar Bear and Other Mammals.* Putnam, 1986. **1569** This beautifully illustrated book shows how easily animals are able to blend into their environments. Also see the other books in this series: *How to Hide a Whippoorwill and Other Birds, How to Hide a Butterfly and Other Insects, How to Hide a Gray Tree Frog and Other Amphibians, How to Hide a Crocodile and Other Reptiles,* and *How to Hide an Octopus and Other Sea Creatures.*	NFI	K–3	I
Heller, Ruth. *The Reason for a Flower.* Putnam, 1983. **1570** The illustrations are works of art that show the variety of flowering plants, methods of pollination, and uses for plants.	NFN	K–6	I
Herberman, Ethan. *The Great Butterfly Hunt: The Mystery of the Migrating Monarchs.* Simon and Schuster, 1990. **1571** The monarch butterfly's migratory habits, studied through scientific observation and analysis, are the focus of this book. Color photographs accompany this research text.	NFI	6–12	P

	Type of literature	Grade span	Illustrations
Herbert, Frank. **Dune.** Ace, 1987.	SF	9–12	
1572 In this science fiction tale, Paul Atrides leads the Freemen of Dune against their galactic enemies. The planet's ecology, culture, religion, and technology are fully described in this book.			
Hickman, Pamela. **Birdwise.** Addison-Wesley, 1989.	NFI	6–12	I
1573 The author presents specific information about birds, birdwatching techniques, and projects to help birds survive.			
Hiller, Ilo. **Introducing the Mammals to Young Naturalists.** Texas A & M, 1990.	NFI	6–12	I
1574 This book includes information about common mammals of the forest, field, and meadow.			
Hirschi, Ron. **Headgear.** Putnam, 1986.	NFN	3–9	P
1575 The author explores the world of animals that have horns or antlers, identifies the characteristics of these animals, and explains the uses of this specific headgear.			
Hirschi, Ron. **Spring.** Dutton, 1990.	F	K–3	P
1576 This book is a poetic and photographic introduction to the wonders of spring in the mountains. Also see the other books in this series: *Fall, Winter,* and *Summer.*			
Hirschi, Ron. **What Is a Bird?** Walker, 1987.	NFI	K–3	P
1577 Color photographs introduce a variety of activities common to birds and in this way define birds for young children. The sequel is *Where Do Birds Live?*			
Hirschi, Ron. **Who Lives in the Forest?** Putnam, 1987.	NFI	K–3	P
1578 This book has clear text and beautiful photographs of forest animals. Also see other books in this series, such as *Who Lives in the Mountains?, Who Lives on the Prairie?,* and *Who Lives in the Alligator Swamp?*			
Hiscock, Bruce. **The Big Tree.** Atheneum, 1991.	NFN	3–6	I
1579 The author intertwines botany and history in telling the story of a seed that is planted in 1775. This seed grows to become a large sugar maple tree. The book covers how trees grow by absorbing and converting nutrients to food and how a tree's bark protects the heartwood.			
Hitching, Francis. **The Neck of the Giraffe.** Dutton, 1983.	NFN	6–12	
1580 This book is a simply written, easily understood discussion of present-day thought concerning evolution. Support for punctuated equilibrium is noted as well as alternatives to Darwinism.			
Hoffman, Stephen M. **What's Under That Rock?*** Atheneum, 1985.	NFI	3–6	I
1581 The author introduces and describes the habits of mollusks, arthropods, amphibians, and reptiles found under rocks and logs in the United States.			
Holling, Holling C. **Minn of the Mississippi.** Houghton Mifflin, 1978.	NFN	3–9	I
1582 This story about the journey of Minn, a snapping turtle, includes information on all types of turtles as well as the history and geography of the Mississippi River area.			

	Type of literature	Grade span	Illustrations

Holling, Holling C. *Pagoo.* Houghton Mifflin, 1990. — F, 3–9, I

1583 The ecosystem of a hermit crab is described through the problems and escapades of Pagoo.

Hooper, Patricia. *A Bundle of Beasts.* Houghton Mifflin, 1987. — P, 9–12

1584 These poems are about the names for groups of different animals: herds, bands, flocks, pods, gaggles, and packs.

Hoover, H. M. *The Rains of Eridan.* Viking, 1977. — SF, 6–12

1585 In this science fiction tale, the humans of Eridan are infected by an irrational fear. Dr. Theodore Leslie, a biologist, discovers both the cause and the cure.

Horner, John K., and James Gorman. *Maia: A Dinosaur Grows Up.* Running Press, 1989. — F, 6–9, I

1586 This story about the possible life of a hatchling dinosaur was inspired by the discovery of the first nesting site of dinosaurs.

Hoshino, Michio. *Grizzly.* Chronicle Books, 1987. — NFN, 9–12, P

1587 The dramatic color shots in this photographic essay portray the environment and daily life of the Alaskan grizzly. Also see *Moose* by Michio Hoshino.

Howe, James. *I Wish I Were a Butterfly.* Harcourt Brace Jovanovich, 1987. — F, K–6, I

1588 With haunting watercolors, the author tells of a cricket who is unhappy with his ugly lot in life and yearns to be a butterfly. One day a butterfly lets him know how very nice it is to hear a cricket.

Hubbell, Sue. *A Book of Bees and How to Keep Them.* Random House, 1988. — NFN, 9–12, I

1589 A beekeeper's personal thoughts cover the four seasons with information on keeping bees.

Hughes, Monica. *The Keeper of the Isis Light.** Atheneum, 1981. — SF, 6–12

1590 In this science fiction tale, settlers from the planet Earth arrive on the planet Isis, and Almen learns the bitter truth about how she has been able to survive in this incredibly harsh world.

Hull, Robert. *Poems for Spring.* Steck-Vaughn, 1991. — P, K–6, I

1591 This is a collection of poems and illustrations that describe spring.

Isberg, Emily. *Peak Performance: Sports, Science, and the Body in Action.* Simon and Schuster, 1989. — NFN, 6–9, P

1592 This book takes an innovative look at the challenges to the performance of individual athletes, who today combine serious training, state-of-the-art equipment, computers, trainers, and sports medicine to develop "peak performance" for both competing and extending their athletic careers.

Isenbart, Hans-Heinrich. *Birth of a Foal.* Carolrhoda, 1986. — NFI, 3–6, P

1593 Color photographs and scientific drawings enhance the descriptions of a foal's birth and early development.

	Type of literature	Grade span	Illus-trations

Isenbart, Hans-Heinrich. *A Duckling Is Born.* Putnam, 1981. — NFI | K–6 | P

1594 Exceptional color photographs introduce a duck's life cycle, the growth and development within an egg, and the hatching process. Information in this book also covers the duck's daily activities and the raising of ducklings.

Jacobs, Francine. *Breakthrough: The True Story of Penicillin.* Dodd, Mead, 1985. — NFI | 6–9 | P

1595 This book covers the history of the extensive research leading to the development of the antibiotic penicillin.

Jastrow, Robert. *The Enchanted Loom.* Simon and Schuster, 1981. — NFI | 6–12

1596 The author outlines the forces behind the evolution of the human species, including the evolution of the human brain, and points out the close parallels between humans' brains and modern computers.

Johanson, Donald E. *Lucy: The Beginnings of Humankind.* Simon and Schuster, 1990. — NFN | 9–12 | P

1597 This is a description of the skeleton of a diminutive female that is, supposedly, the oldest one unearthed in Africa. Some of the ideas presented in this book are controversial.

Johnson, Rebecca. *The Greenhouse Effect: Life on a Warmer Planet.* Lerner, 1990. — NFI | 6–12 | P

1598 This book addresses the causes and effects of the greenhouse phenomenon on the world environment. The author explains how current research methods are used to gather, measure, and compare data. [Ecology]

Johnson, Rebecca. *The Secret Language: Pheromones in the Animal World.* Lerner, 1989. — NFI | 6–9 | P

1599 This is an introduction to the way animals and insects communicate with their own kind by producing and releasing certain chemicals known as pheromones.

Johnson, Sylvia A. *Bats.* Lerner, 1985. — NFI | 3–9 | P

1600 Enchanting pictures illustrate the varieties, characteristics, and behaviors of bats and their young. Also discussed are their contributions to the environment and recommendations for their protection.

Johnson, Sylvia A. *Beetles.* Lerner, 1982. — NFI | 3–9 | P

1601 This introduction to beetles covers their extensive varieties, their physical characteristics, and their life cycles. Also see the other books in this series, such as *Wasps, Mantises, Butterflies, Fireflies, Water Insects,* and *Silkworms.*

Johnson, Sylvia A. *Crabs.* Lerner, 1982. — NFI | 3–9 | P

1602 This introduction to crabs has wonderful pictures that show the varieties, the physical characteristics, and the life cycles of these crustaceans.

Johnson, Sylvia A. *Elephant Seals.* Lerner, 1989. — NFI | 3–9 | P

1603 Wonderful pictures help to introduce elephant seals, including their physical characteristics, mating rituals, and the growth and development of the pups. Current research and conservation efforts are also discussed. Also see other books in this series, such as *Penguins.*

	Type of literature	Grade span	Illus- trations

Johnson, Sylvia A. *Hermit Crabs.* Lerner, 1989.

1604 Wonderful pictures and scientific drawings introduce hermit crabs and illustrate their environments, life cycles, physical characteristics, and partnerships with sea anemones.

| | NFI | 3–9 | P |

Johnson, Sylvia A. *How Leaves Change.* Lerner, 1986.

1605 The life cycles of leaves are explored, from their formation to their disintegration into soil nutrients. Beautiful color photographs accompany lucid explanations of processes such as photosynthesis, color change, and abscission.

| | NFI | K–6 | P |

Johnson, Sylvia A. *Inside an Egg.* Lerner, 1982.

1606 Fascinating color photographs and illustrations of an egg's interior show the growth, development, and hatching of a chick embryo.

| | NFI | 3–9 | P |

Johnson, Sylvia A. *Morning Glories.* Lerner, 1985.

1607 Morning glory plants are introduced with explicit pictures and scientific drawings that illustrate this plant's seeds, development, and blooming patterns. Comparisons are made to other plants.

| | NFI | 3–9 | P |

Johnson, Sylvia A. *Mushrooms.* Lerner, 1982.

1608 Beautiful pictures of mushrooms and other fungi show how they reproduce and illustrate their role in the cycle of natural life. Also see other books in this series, such as *Mosses*.

| | NFI | 3–9 | P |

Johnson, Sylvia A. *Potatoes.* Lerner, 1984.

1609 This absorbing book introduces the potato plant and points out its importance as food for humans. The varieties of potatoes are described, as is their development, cultivation, growth, and harvesting.

| | NFI | 3–9 | P |

Johnson, Sylvia A. *Rice.* Lerner, 1985.

1610 This introduction to the rice plant covers its history, importance, development, cultivation, growth patterns, harvest, and value as food.

| | NFI | 3–9 | P |

Johnson, Sylvia A. *Snails.* Lerner, 1982.

1611 Land snails (gastropod mollusks) are the subjects of scientific drawings and color pictures that show physical characteristics, life cycle, place in the food chain, reproduction methods, habits, and habitats.

| | NFI | 3–9 | P |

Johnson, Sylvia A. *Snakes.* Lerner, 1986.

1612 Snakes are introduced with arresting pictures and scientific drawings that enhance the descriptions of the varieties, their physical characteristics, abilities, habitats, life cycles, and hatching of the young.

| | NFI | 3–9 | P |

Johnson, Sylvia A. *Tree Frogs.* Lerner, 1986.

1613 Pictures and text describe the forest tree frog, an intriguing amphibian with the ability to change colors. Some varieties actually lay their eggs in trees.

| | NFI | 3–9 | P |

Johnson, Sylvia A. *Wolf Pack: Tracking Wolves in the Wild.* Lerner, 1985.

1614 This introduction to wolves covers their physical and social characteristics, the development and growth of their pups, and the methods scientists use to study them.

| | NFI | 3–9 | P |

	Type of literature	Grade span	Illustrations

Johnston, Ginny, and Judy Cutchins. *Scaly Babies: Reptiles Growing Up.* William Morrow, 1988. — NFI — 3–6 — P

1615 Color photographs show the hatching of a variety of reptiles, such as snakes, lizards, alligators, and turtles. The text traces their struggles to survive.

Kilpatrick, Cathy. *Creepy Crawlies: Insects and Other Tiny Animals.* Usborne, 1990. — NFI — K–6 — I

1616 This book defines land invertebrates and compares them to similar living things. The illustrations enhance and clarify the facts about these creatures.

Kitchen, Bert. *Animal Alphabet.* Dial, 1984. — NFI — K–3 — I

1617 The stylized creatures in this alphabet book create a desire to know their names and more about them as they introduce the alphabet.

Knapp, Toni. *The Six Bridges of Humphrey the Whale.* Rockrimmon, 1989. — NFN — 3–6 — I

1618 Watercolor illustrations help tell about the adventures of this humpback whale who swam across the San Francisco Bay and into the waters of the Sacramento Delta before he was rescued and returned to the Pacific Ocean.

Koestler, Arthur. *The Case of the Midwife Toad.* Random House, 1971. — NFN — 9–12 — I

1619 This book is the result of Koestler's research into the life of Austrian biologist Paul Kammerer, whose published findings on the midwife toad supported a Lamarckian view of genetics. Outraged neo-Darwinists "proved" him wrong, and Kammerer committed suicide. Koestler's book is, in part, a vindication.

Kohl, Judith, and Herbert Kohl. *The View from the Oak.* Sierra /Scribner, 1977. — NFN — 6–12 — S

1620 This book is an introduction to the perspective and reactions of a variety of animals. [Ecology]

Krutch, Joseph Wood. *The Great Chain of Life.* Houghton Mifflin, 1978. — NFN — 6–12

1621 This book is a collection of introspective essays on the life sciences.

Landau, Elaine. *Alzheimer's Disease.* Franklin Watts, 1987. — NFI — 6–12

1622 This book provides medical insight into this degenerative disease. It also reveals how different family members feel about coping with this illness and how they cope with the death of the Alzheimer sufferer.

Lane, Margaret. *The Fish: The Story of the Stickleback.* Dial, 1981. — NFI — 3–9 — I

1623 This enchanting book introduces the unusual mating habits of the common stickleback fish.

Lauber, Patricia. *From Flower to Flower: Animals and Pollination.* Crown Publishers, 1987. — NFI — 6–9 — P

1624 In this book about flower pollination, the text is enhanced by excellent black-and-white photographs.

Lauber, Patricia. *The News About Dinosaurs.* Bradbury, 1989. — NFI — 3–9 — P

1625 This book features current research on and knowledge of dinosaurs, with photographs and illustrations from 1870 through 1988.

	Type of literature	Grade span	Illus- trations

Lauber, Patricia. *Sea Otters and Seaweed.* Garrard, 1976.

    1626 This classic book describes the ecosystem needed by the California sea otter. The role and value of the sea otters in maintaining the balance of life in the kelp forest is discussed. [Ecology]

    NFI 3–6 P

Lauber, Patricia. *Tales Mummies Tell.* Harper, 1985.

    1627 This book describes the scientific study of mummies found in Egypt, Peru, and Europe and reveals what scientists have learned about ancient civilizations. Both natural mummies and those preserved through embalming are discussed.

    NFI 6–9 P

Lauber, Patricia. *What's Hatching out of That Egg?* Crown Publishers, 1991.

    1628 As photographs invite the reader to guess what kind of creature might be hatching from a variety of eggs, the text describes each creature.

    NFI K–3 P

Lavies, Bianca. *Backyard Hunter: The Praying Mantis.* Dutton, 1990.

    1629 Marvelous color photographs illustrate the life cycle of the praying mantis. The pictures start with the hatching of an egg case; are followed by molting, hunting, and mating; and end with the building of a new egg case.

    NFI 3–6 P

Lavies, Bianca. *It's an Armadillo.* Dutton, 1989.

    1630 Outstanding color photographs introduce the elusive nine-banded armadillo, illustrating its physical characteristics, life style, habitat, and rearing of its young.

    NFI 3–6 P

Lavies, Bianca. *Lily Pad Pond.* Dutton, 1989.

    1631 Exceptional color photographs illustrate the tadpole's development into a frog. Also included in the pictures are some of the other creatures that share the pond and are part of the food chain. [Ecology]

    NFI K–3 P

Lavies, Bianca. *Secretive Timber Rattlesnakes.* Dutton, 1990.

    1632 Dramatic full-color pictures follow the snake as it sheds its skin, hibernates in deep underground caves, hunts, kills, and swallows its prey.

    NFI 3–6 P

Lavies, Bianca. *Tree Trunk Traffic.* Dutton, 1989.

    1633 In this simple story a young, busy squirrel family is the focal point that connects the various navigators along the tree trunk. [Ecology]

    NFN K–3 P

Lavine, Sigmund A. *Wonders of Woodchucks.* Dodd, Mead, 1984.

    1634 This book includes factual information about the woodchuck's biology, activities, and environment. Also included are several legends about wood-chucks.

    NFI 3–9 P

Lawrence, Louise. *Children of the Dust.* Harper, 1985.

    1635 This is a fictional look at what might happen after a nuclear devastation and how the survivors might adapt physically and emotionally. This tale follows the survivors and their descendants through three generations.

    SF 6–9

Lawrence, R. D. *Wolves.* Little, Brown, 1990.

    1636 This book has outstanding photographs and sketches of wolves and a detailed text on their behavior and their place in the natural environment.

    NFI 3–6 P

	Type of literature	Grade span	Illus- trations

Leakey, L. S. B. *By the Evidence: Memoirs, 1932–1951.* Harcourt Brace Jovanovich, 1974.

1637 The renown anthropologist recounts his life and his field work from 1932 to 1951.

NFN   9–12

Leakey, Richard. *Human Origins.* Dutton, 1982.

1638 From fossils, skeletons, cave drawings, and other artifacts, the author describes and traces the origins of human life and of its evolution.

NFN   6–12

Leatherwood, Stephan, and Randall Reeves. *The Sea World Book of Dolphins.* Harcourt Brace Jovanovich, 1987.

1639 The various types of dolphins are described and photographed by the authors. They also include information about dolphins' physical characteristics, habits, and natural environments.

NFI   3–9   P

LeGuin, Ursula. *The Left Hand of Darkness.* Ace, 1983.

1640 In this science fiction tale, humans in the world of Winter are hermaphroditic and have developed a society that is not based on gender. An envoy from the galactic community becomes embroiled in their lives and must reconsider his attitudes about human identity and relationships.

SF   9–12

Leopold, Aldo. *A Sand Country Almanac: And Sketches Here and There.* Oxford, 1949.

1641 This classic book was one of the first to plead for protection of the environment. One would think that these essays about the decline of natural populations and the plundering of the land by industry and homeowners had been written recently. [Ecology]

NFN   9–12   I

Lerner, Carol. *A Forest Year.* William Morrow, 1987.

1642 This book provides a season-by-season description of the inhabitants of a northeastern forest ecosystem. The beautiful illustrations show cross sections above and below ground and are labeled for easy identification.

NFN   6–9   I

Lerner, Carol. *On the Forest Edge.* William Morrow, 1978.

1643 The author introduces the varied and numerous populations of plants, birds, and animals whose habitats are the unmowed borders usually found along roads.

NFN   3–6   I

Leslie-Melville, Betty. *Daisy Rothschild.* Doubleday, 1987.

1644 The author uses the baby giraffe named Daisy Rothschild to tell the story of the endangered Rothschild giraffe species and to discuss conservation efforts in Africa.

NFN   3–6   P

Leslie-Melville, Betty. *Walter Warthog.* Doubleday, 1989.

1645 Important information is provided about African wildlife and conservation efforts as the author tells the story of a Nairobi warthog that joins her family.

NFN   3–6   P

Lester, Alison. *Imagine.* Houghton Mifflin, 1990.

1646 This book encourages children to use their imaginations as they follow the adventures of a young boy and girl who visit different ecosystems around the world and observe the animals who inhabit each one.

NFN   K–3   I

Livingston, Myra Cohn. *Circle of Seasons.* Holiday House, 1982.

1647 Charming light poems and delightful illustrations present each season, starting with spring.

P   K–6   I

	Type of literature	Grade span	Illustrations
Livingston, Myra Cohn. *Monkey Puzzle and Other Poems.* E. M. McElderry, 1984. **1648** Plants and trees are the focus in this poetry collection.	P	3–6	I
London, Jack. *Call of the Wild.* Scholastic, 1987. **1649** This classic novel is about a dog who becomes the leader of a Klondike wolf pack.	F	6–12	
London, Jack. *White Fang.* Scholastic, 1986. **1650** In this classic story a wild wolf-dog is tamed with kindness and love.	F	6–12	
Maass, Robert. *When Autumn Comes.* Holt, Rinehart and Winston, 1990. **1651** This is a photographic essay that looks at autumn in the country. The simple text describes how both the people and the animals prepare for winter.	NFI	K–3	P
Mabey, Richard. *Oak and Company.* Greenwillow, 1983. **1652** An oak tree's life is recounted from its beginnings as an acorn to its death over 200 years later. The animals and the plants that share this tree's ecosystem are part of its life story.	NFI	3–6	I
MacClintock, Dorcas. *Phoebe the Kinkajou.** Scribner's, 1985. **1653** The author describes a kinkajou's life as it adapts from the tropical rain forest to a research laboratory and, finally, to a home with a human family. Also included is information about kinkajous' physical characteristics and native habitats.	NFN	3–6	P
McClung, Robert. *How Animals Hide.* National Geographic Society, 1973. **1654** Color photographs and an easy text describe the different ways that animals use camouflage both to protect themselves and to obtain food.	NFI	3–6	P
McCutcheon, Marc. *The Compass in Your Nose, and Other Astonishing Facts About Humans.* Tarcher, 1989. **1655** This book, a compendium of fascinating facts about the human body, is illustrated with cartoons that make the information more understandable.	NFI	6–12	I
MacDonald, David. *Running with the Fox.* Facts on File, 1988. **1656** Excellent photographs and sketches of foxes accompany these warm, detailed notes written by a researcher who is an authority on foxes. Sprinkled throughout this book are sidebars that address such questions as "Are foxes good pets?"	NFN	9–12	P
McDonald, Megan. *Is This a House for Hermit Crab?* Orchard, 1990. **1657** The illustrations help convey a hermit crab's efforts to find the perfect shell to use as a new home.	F	K–3	I
McKibben, Bill. *The End of Nature.* Doubleday, 1990. **1658** The impact of humans on the environment is documented in this plea to rethink what we have done and continue to do to our "terrestrial ark." The author supports his position with statistics, proposing a simpler way of living. [Ecology]	NFN	9–12	
McLaughlin, Molly. *Dragonflies.* Walker, 1989. **1659** The author discusses the origins of dragonflies, as well as the environment necessary for their survival. Exquisite close-up photographs of both dragonflies and damselflies point up their similarities and differences.	NFI	3–9	P

	Type of literature	Grade span	Illustrations

McLaughlin, Molly. *Earthworms, Dirt, and Rotten Leaves: An Exploration in Ecology.* Macmillan, 1986. — NFI, 3–9, I

1660 This book presents facts about earthworms and the important role they play. It suggests experiments that introduce basic ecological concepts and includes an "earthworm observation guide" that could easily be adapted to the observation of other animals. [Ecology]

McLoughlin, John C. *Archosauria: A New Look at the Old Dinosaur.* Viking, 1979. — NFN, 6–12, I

1661 The author incorporates recent theories and descriptions of dinosaur anatomy and physiology based on recent digs as he presents startling theories of warm-blooded dinosaurs that are maternal and nurturing.

McPhee, John. *Coming into the Country.* Farrar, Straus and Giroux, 1991. — NFI, 9–12

1662 The personal stories of immigrants to Alaska reflect their courage and endurance, their observations of wildlife, and the nature of fishing above the Arctic Circle. The book concludes with a discussion of the issues currently facing Alaska's residents.

McPhee, John. *Oranges.* Farrar, Straus and Giroux, 1967. — NFN, 6–12, I

1663 This is the definitive work on the orange, including its history; its botanical characteristics; its manufacture into juice and other products; and sketches of the men and women who grow, pick, and process this fruit.

Maddern, Eric. *Life Story.* Barron's, 1988. — NFN, K–6, I

1664 The author is a combination storyteller, scientist, and artist who brings the story of evolution within easy reach. This book begins with the first living cells and moves across time from fish to reptiles, birds, and humans.

Madison, Arnold. *Drugs and You* (Revised edition). Edited by Jane Stelten Pohl. Julian Messner, 1990. — NFI, 3–6, P

1665 The classes of drugs, their uses, and their effects on the human body are explained. This comprehensive book would make an excellent sourcebook.

Maestro, Betsy. *A Sea Full of Sharks.* Scholastic, 1990. — NF, 3–6, I

1666 This detailed and beautifully illustrated book compares and contrasts the many kinds of sharks and explains the reasons scientists find them fascinating.

Malnig, Anita. *Where the Waves Break: Life at the Edge of the Sea.* Lerner, 1987. — NFI, 3–6, P

1667 Sea creatures and plants found in tidepools and near the shore are introduced in this book that includes both beautiful photographs and the scientific names of the plants and animals. [Ecology]

Matthews, Downs. *Polar Bear Cubs.* Simon and Schuster, 1991. — NFI, 3–6, P

1668 The daily life of twin polar bear cubs is described and illustrated with a series of photographs taken of them and their mother over two years

Mellonie, Bryan, and Robert Ingpen. *Lifetimes: The Beautiful Way to Explain Death to Children.* Bantam, 1983. — NFN, K–6, I

1669 The illustrations of insects, animals, people, and plants sensitively convey the idea that the lifetime of each living thing has a beginning and an ending.

	Type of literature	Grade span	Illus-trations
Meltzer, Milton. *The Landscape of Memory.* Viking, 1987. **1670** This work is an accessible look at the physiology of the human mind and how memory works on personal, cultural, and historical levels.	NFI	6–9	
Meyers, Susan. *Pearson: A Harbor Seal Pup.* Dutton, 1980. **1671** A California harbor seal pup is rescued, cared for, and finally returned to the wild in this true story.	NFN	3–9	P
Miles, Betty. *Save the Earth: An Action Handbook for Kids.* Knopf, 1991. **1672** This is a wonderfully informative book concerning the many environmental problems we face today. The author also suggests techniques that have worked for others to help solve these problems. [Ecology]	NFR	3–6	P
Miller, Jonathan. *Darwin for Beginners.* Pantheon, 1982. **1673** This is an accessible, amusing look at Charles Darwin's theories and work that is presented in a comic book format.	NFN	9–12	I
Miller, Jonathan. *The Human Body.* Viking, 1983. **1674** With realistic pop-up and movable illustrations of the head, body cavity, heart, joints, and muscles, this book provides a fascinating peek inside the human body.	NFI	6–9	I
Milne, Lorus J., and Margery Milne. *A Shovelful of Earth.* Henry Holt, 1987. **1675** This investigation of the soils of several biomes reveals how different animals have adapted to them.	NFI	6–12	S
Milne, Lorus J., and Margery Milne. *The Mystery of the Bog Forest.* Dodd, Mead, 1984. **1676** This book describes the complex ecosystem found in the acidic environment of a bog and the many life forms it supports, from the sundew plant to orchids and cranberries [Ecology]	NFI	6–9	
Montgomery, Sy. *Walking with the Great Apes: Jane Goodall, Diane Fossey, Birute Galdikas.* Houghton Mifflin, 1991. **1677** This investigative scientist and journalist shares her love of wild animals with the three extraordinary women who devote their lives to studying and researching chimpanzees, mountain gorillas, and orangutans.	B	9–12	
Moorehead, Alan. *Darwin and the Beagle.* Harper, 1969. **1678** This biography includes insight into Darwin's relationship with the captain of the *Beagle,* the locations the ship visited, and descriptions of the specimens Darwin collected.	B	6–9	I
Moss, Cynthia. *Elephant Memories: Thirteen Years in the Life of an Elephant Family.* William Morrow, 1988. **1679** The author warmly describes her research study on the elephant population in Amboseli National Park, Kenya.	NFN	9–12	
Mowat, Farley. *Never Cry Wolf.* Bantam, 1983. **1680** In this narration the author describes the wild wolves of Canada's frozen tundra and his own journey to a deep and abiding respect for these animals. [Ecology]	NFN	6–12	

	Type of literature	Grade span	Illus- trations

Mowat, Farley. *Owls in the Family.* Bantam, 1985.
1681 This is the story of two young orphaned owls that are rescued, join a human family, and participate in many delightful adventures.
F — **3–6** — **I**

Mowat, Farley. *A Whale for the Killing.* Bantam, 1984.
1682 Based on a real-life incident, this book describes the senseless killing of whales. [Ecology]
NFN — **6–12**

Mowat, Farley. *Woman in the Mists: The Story of Diane Fossey and the Mountain Gorillas of Africa.* Warner, 1987.
1683 Excerpts from Diane Fossey's journal fill Mowat's account of her study of the mountain gorilla. He uses her own words to describe her battle against the poachers who killed these gentle creatures and who, it is believed, murdered her.
B — **9–12** — **P**

Murphy, Jim. *The Call of the Wolves.* Scholastic, 1989.
1684 Beautiful illustrations enhance this story about a young arctic wolf's adventures before he is able to return to his pack. This book includes a short history and a list of additional readings on wolves.
F — **3–6** — **I**

Mutel, Cornelia F., and Mary M. Rodgers. *Our Endangered Planet: Tropical Rain Forests.* Lerner, 1991.
1685 The importance of rain forests and their effects on the atmosphere are covered in this book that includes environmental projects. [Ecology]
NFI — **6–9** — **P**

National Geographic Society Staff. *Amazing Animals of Australia.* National Geographic Society, 1984.
1686 The subject of this book is the natural history of Australia's amazing assortment of animals.
NFN — **3–9** — **P**

National Geographic Society Staff. *Living on Earth.* National Geographic Society, 1988.
1687 Impressive photography shows both the interaction of native peoples with their environment and biomes. [Ecology]
NFI — **6–12** — **P**

Naylor, Phyllis. *Beetles, Lightly Toasted.* Dell, 1987.
1688 A farm boy plans to win the conservation contest by developing recipes using bugs and worms, but he needs taste tests for his research project. The excitement starts when he serves these unique foods without mentioning the secret ingredients.
F — **3–6**

Newton, James R. *A Forest Is Reborn.* Harper, 1982.
1689 A forest's rejuvenation after a fire is described in this book. [Ecology]
NFI — **3–6** — **I**

Nickerson, Roy. *Sea Otters: A Natural History and Guide* (Revised edition). Chronicle Books, 1989.
1690 Pertinent information regarding the natural history of sea otters is covered in this book, as well as the conflict between those who fish for a living and conservationists.
NFI — **6–12** — **P**

Nilsson, Lennart. *Behold, Man.* Little, Brown, 1978.
1691 The formation, functions, and interrelationships among the cells, tissues, and organs of the human body are the subjects of this book. Colored micrographs enhance the text.
NFI — **9–12** — **P**

	Type of literature	Grade span	Illus-trations
Nilsson, Lennart. *A Child Is Born.* Dell, 1986. **1692** The text is enhanced by graphic *in utero* photographs showing neonatal development, the birth process, and finally a newborn baby. This book is for the serious student. Note: See California *Education Code,* Section 51550, regarding sex education.	NFI	6–12	P
Nilsson, Lennart. *Close to Nature: An Exploration of Nature's Microcosm.* Pantheon, 1984. **1693** Striking full-color photographs underscore a text that describes plants and animals at very close range.	NFI	6–12	P
Nolan, Dennis. *Wolf Child.* Macmillan Children's Book Group, 1989. **1694** The relationship between humans and animals is depicted in this story set in the Ice Age. A boy rescues, loves, and raises a small orphan wolf cub that then saves the lives of the boy and the clan leader.	F	6–9	I
North, Sterling. *The Wolfling.* Scholastic, 1980. **1695** Robbie's greatest wish is to find a wolfling to raise. This is the story of his dream coming true.	F	6–9	I
O'Brien, Robert. *Z for Zachariah.* Collier Books for Young Adults, 1987. **1696** In this science fiction tale, a young girl adjusts to being the sole survivor of a nuclear war. Then a strange man appears, and her lonely but peaceful existence is threatened.	SF	6–9	
O'Dell, Scott. *Island of the Blue Dolphins.* Dell, 1987. **1697** This story is based on the life of a young American Indian girl who lives alone on her island home for 18 years before she is rescued. By that time she has become attuned to nature and to the creatures who also live on the island before her rescue.	F	3–6	
Oppenheim, Joanne. *Have You Seen Birds?* Scholastic, 1988. **1698** Birds are depicted in various seasonal activities. The creative illustrations are colorful clay-relief pictures of birds.	NFN	K–3	I
Overbeck, Cynthia. *Ants.* Lerner, 1982. **1699** The ants' life cycle, physical characteristics, social structures, and ecosystems are introduced with a clear text and detailed, enlarged photographs. Another book to see from this series is *Dragonflies*.	NFI	3–9	P
Overbeck, Cynthia. *Cactus.* Lerner, 1982. **1700** This book is about the plants that are able to survive in and adapt to a desert environment. The differences between cactus and succulents and their relationship to other flowering plants are explained.	NFI	3–9	P
Overbeck, Cynthia. *Carnivorous Plants.* Lerner, 1982. **1701** The luring methods of both active and passive meat-eating plants are discussed and illustrated by colorful photographs.	NFI	3–9	P
Overbeck, Cynthia. *Cats.* Lerner, 1983. **1702** The physical characteristics and behaviors of the domestic cat are compared to those of its wild relatives.	NFI	3–9	P
Overbeck, Cynthia. *Elephants.* Lerner, 1981. **1703** Excellent photographs introduce elephants, along with detailed descriptions of their ecosystem.	NFI	3–9	P

	Type of literature	Grade span	Illustrations

Overbeck, Cynthia. *How Seeds Travel.* Lerner, 1982.

    1704 This book describes seed dispersal by animals, wind, and water. The movement of seeds over a wide area is shown in photographs using both common and uncommon seeds.

    NFI   3–9   P

Overbeck, Cynthia. *Lions.* Lerner, 1981.

    1705 This book is an introduction to the life cycle and ecosystem of lions.

    NFI   3–9   P

Overbeck, Cynthia. *Monkeys.* Lerner, 1981.

    1706 The life of the Japanese macaques on the island of Honshu is detailed in this book. It includes information on their family life, habits, and ability to survive in a climate that includes snowfalls and freezing weather.

    NFI   3–9   P

Overbeck, Cynthia. *Sunflowers.* Lerner, 1981.

    1707 The sunflower's development and growth are followed from a seed to a mature flower. Close-up photographs show the parts of the flower, pollination, and fertilization.

    NFI   3–9   P

Oxford Scientific Films Staff. *House Mouse.* Putnam, 1978.

    1708 Wonderful photographs introduce this mouse and illustrate its feeding habits, nest building, and care of its young. This series also includes the book *Harvest Mouse.*

    NFI   K–6   P

Oxford Scientific Films Staff. *Side by Side.* Edited by Miranda MacQuitty. Putnam, 1988.

    1709 Symbiosis is introduced with large color photographs that enhance the text. Another book to see in this series is *Dragonflys over the Water.*

    NFI   3–6   P

Oxford Scientific Films Staff. *The Wild Rabbit.* Putnam, 1980.

    1710 The wild European rabbit is introduced with information about its habitat, physical characteristics, life cycle, mating, and the care of its young.

    NFI   K–6   P

Pace, Mildred Mastin. *Wrapped for Eternity: The Story of the Egyptian Mummy.* McGraw-Hill, 1974.

    1711 The author takes a scientific and historical look at the mummification process, emphasizing the Egyptian mummy.

    NFI   6–12   P

Page, Jake. *Zoo: The Modern Ark.* Facts on File, 1990.

    1712 Today zoos are much more than just a place for humans to view exotic animals: they are the breeding grounds for endangered animals. As the author points out, zoos are often the only hope for the survival of some species.

    NFN   9–12   P

Pallotta, Jerry. *The Bird Alphabet Book.* Charlesbridge, 1989.

    1713 Large, colorful, detailed drawings and simple facts introduce 26 different species of birds.

    NFI   3–6   I

Parker, Nancy Winslow. *Frogs, Toads, Lizards, and Salamanders.* Greenwillow, 1990.

    1714 This book is an excellent introduction to the study of amphibians, with its scientific drawings, interesting facts, and pun-type riddles.

    NFN   K–6   S

Parker, Nancy Winslow, and Joan R. Wright. *Bugs.* William Morrow, 1988.

    1715 Sixteen bugs are profiled in this book with descriptions that include general information about each. Large, detailed scientific drawings accompany each description.

    NFI   K–6   S

	Type of literature	Grade span	Illus-trations
Parker, Steve. *Pond and River.* Knopf, 1988. **1716** Fresh-water plants, animals, fish, and shells are introduced with information pertinent to each species. The color photographs make comparisons of species easy.	NFI	3–9	P
Parker, Steve. *Seashore.* Knopf, 1989. **1717** The creatures and plants that inhabit seashores are introduced with detailed color photographs. The last chapter discusses the importance of preserving our shores.	NFI	3–9	P
Parker, Steve. *Skeleton.* Knopf, 1988. **1718** Evolution, structure, and the function of human and animal skeletons are introduced in this book. Skeletons are easy to study in the detailed pictures that compare herbivores and carnivores; shells and armor; and arms, wings, and flippers.	NFI	3–9	P
Parnall, Peter. *Apple Tree.* Macmillan Children's Book Group, 1988. **1719** The author describes his old apple tree, and the insects and birds that are a part of its ecosystem, through the seasons.	NFN	3–6	I
Parnall, Peter. *Daywatchers.* Macmillan, 1984. **1720** These narrative essays describing American hawks are beautifully illustrated by the author's black-and-white drawings.	NFN	3–9	I
Parnall, Peter. *A Dog's Book of Birds.** Scribner's, 1977. **1721** A wide variety of birds are presented in short, quick phrases from a dog's viewpoint.	NFN	3–9	I
Parnall, Peter. *Quiet.* William Morrow, 1989. **1722** The author describes all of the interesting things that might happen when you place food on your chest and lie very quietly in the woods.	NFN	K–6	I
Parsons, Alexandra. *Amazing Cats.* Knopf, 1991. **1723** The concise, interesting text and color photographs and illustrations provide many facts about both wild and tame cats. Also see other books in the JUNIOR EYEWITNESS series.	NFI	3–6	I
Parsons, Alexandra. *Amazing Poisonous Animals.* Knopf, 1991. **1724** Wonderful photographs and illustrations feature the poisonous creatures of the world. The text gives a concise history and description of each creature.	NFI	3–6	I
Patent, Dorothy Hinshaw. *Buffalo: The American Bison Today.* Ticknor and Fields, 1986. **1725** The American bison is introduced, as well as the ecosystem needed to maintain this historically important animal. [Ecology]	NFI	3–9	P
Patent, Dorothy Hinshaw. *Mosquitoes.* Holiday House, 1986. **1726** Close-up photographs accompany explanations of mosquitoes' life cycles and feeding patterns. Also discussed are malaria parasites and methods to eliminate biting mosquitoes.	NFI	3–9	P
Patent, Dorothy Hinshaw. *Quarter Horses.* Holiday House, 1985. **1727** The author discusses the quarter horse's origins, its natural talents and abilities, and its importance to humans. Another book to see by this author is *Thoroughbred Horses.*	NFI	3–9	P

	Type of literature	Grade span	Illustrations
Patent, Dorothy Hinshaw. *Sizes and Shapes in Nature: What They Mean.* Holiday House, 1979. **1728** The factors that influence both the size and shape of animals and plants are examined in this book.	NFI	3–9	S
Patent, Dorothy Hinshaw. *Spider Magic.* Holiday House, 1982. **1729** This introduction to 12 different kinds of spiders includes general information about their physical characteristics and webs. Also see *The Lives of Spiders* by this author.	NFI	3–9	P
Patent, Dorothy Hinshaw. *Whales: Giants of the Deep.* Holiday House, 1984. **1730** The varieties of whales are presented in this book that discusses their physical and social characteristics, their importance to humans, and recent conservation efforts in their behalf. Also see other books in this series, including *Humpback Whales* and *Dolphins and Porpoises.*	NFI	3–9	P
Patent, Dorothy Hinshaw. *Wheat: The Golden Harvest.* Putnam, 1987. **1731** The history and development of wheat are described in this book that also discusses its cultivation and importance as food.	NFI	3–9	P
Patent, Dorothy Hinshaw. *Where the Bald Eagles Gather.* Houghton Mifflin, 1990. **1732** This book describes the research methods and techniques of the scientists who study the eagles that annually feed on spawning salmon in Glacier National Park, Montana.	NFI	3–9	P
Patent, Dorothy Hinshaw. *The Whooping Crane: A Comeback Story.* Ticknor and Fields, 1988. **1733** The whooping crane's history and scientists' efforts to save this species from extinction are described in this book.	NFI	3–9	P
Patent, Dorothy Hinshaw. *Wild Turkey, Tame Turkey.* Houghton Mifflin, 1989. **1734** The author explains the differences between wild and domesticated turkeys. Turkey farming is also discussed.	NFI	3–9	P
Patterson, Francine. *Koko's Story.* Scholastic, 1988. **1735** The author describes the daily life and education of the gorilla Koko, who is learning sign language. This author also wrote *Koko's Kitten.*	NFN	K–6	P
Paulsen, Gary. *Hatchet.* Puffin, 1988. **1736** In this novel a boy survives in the Canadian wilderness for 54 days with only his clothes and a small hatchet.	F	6–9	
Paulsen, Gary. *The Island.* Dell, 1990. **1737** In this novel twelve-year-old William is drawn to an island's rustic beauty that makes him feel a part of nature.	F	6–12	
Paulsen, Gary. *Woodsong.* Macmillan, 1990. **1738** The author describes competing in the Alaskan Iditarod and observes the tenuous connections among nature, animals, and humans.	B	6–12	
Peck, Robert Newton. *A Day No Pigs Would Die.* Dell, 1979. **1739** A young Shaker farm boy learns the meaning of life, death, manhood, and courage in this novel.	F	6–9	

	Type of literature	Grade span	Illustrations
Peters, David. *From the Beginning: The Story of Human Evolution.* William Morrow, 1991. **1740** The author traces the history of life and human evolution in this book. The scientific drawings are especially helpful.	NFI	6–9	S
Powzyk, Joyce. *Tasmania: A Wildlife Journey.* Lothrop, Lee and Shepard, 1987. **1741** The author introduces Tasmanian creatures and environment. Watercolors enhance the descriptive text.	NFI	3–6	I
Powzyk, Joyce. *Tracking Wild Chimpanzees.* Lothrop, Lee and Shepard, 1988. **1742** Watercolors illustrate life in the rain forest as the author describes the birds, animals, and plants she encounters there. She also discusses the importance of preserving rain forests.	NFI	3–6	I
Pringle, Laurence. *Death Is Natural.* William Morrow, 1991. **1743** The author discusses death by describing what happens when a wild rabbit is killed. He discusses the effects of the scavengers and then the bacteria. He explains what is happening at a molecular level and describes the release of energy and the recycling of nutrients.	NFN	3–9	P
Pringle, Laurence. *Restoring Our Earth.* Enslow, 1987. **1744** The author describes lands that have recently been restored or reclaimed, such as marshlands, lakes, rivers, forests, and lands damaged by strip mining. [Ecology]	NFI	6–9	I
Quammen, David. *Flight of the Iguana: A Sidelong View of Science and Nature.* Delacorte, 1988. **1745** With wit and humor, the author identifies and explains a variety of unusual "daily phenomena" and scientific riddles in the natural world.	NFN	9–12	I
Rahn, Joan Elma. *Ears, Hearing, and Balance.** Atheneum, 1984. **1746** The physics of sound is explored in this book, which also describes the structure and function of ears in human beings and other hearing animals.	NFI	6–9	I
Rawls, Wilson. *Summer of the Monkeys.* Dell, 1977. **1747** This story is about a boy living in rural Oklahoma at the turn of the century. His attempts to capture some missing monkeys result in his learning much about nature and about himself.	F	6–9	
Rawls, Wilson. *Where the Red Fern Grows.* Bantam, 1974. **1748** This classic describes a boy's raccoon-hunting adventures and his interesting interactions with other wild animals.	F	6–9	
Readers' Digest Editors. *Sharks: Silent Hunters of the Deep.* Readers' Digest, 1987. **1749** This compendium of information on sharks includes historical references, from ancient times to the present, as well as current research on sharks' behavior. The book also includes charts, maps, data on shark attacks, and myriad photographs.	NFI	6–12	P
Reed, Don C. *Sevengill: The Shark and Me.* Scholastic, 1987. **1750** This life story of a sevengill shark includes safety tips for divers and swimmers.	NFN	3–6	I

	Type of literature	Grade span	Illus- trations

Ricciuti, Edward. *To the Brink of Extinction.* Harper and Row, 1974.
1751 Seven animals that face extinction are described, and factors that influence extinction are discussed.

	NFN	9–12	

Riedman, Marianne. *Sea Otters.* Monterey Bay Aquarium, 1990.
1752 All facets of this fascinating animal are explored by the author in the text and in photographs.

	NFN	6–9	P

Riedman, Sarah R. *Biological Clocks.* Crowell, 1982.
1753 Explaining that all living things live by internal "clocks" that are linked to the rhythms of the earth and the moon, the author clarifies how internal rhythms are set and what happens when they are distorted and need to be reset.

	NFI	6–12	S

Rights, Mollie. *Beastly Neighbors: All About Wild Things in the City, or Why Earwigs Make Good Mothers.* Little, Brown, 1981.
1754 The activities and explorations in this book introduce the bugs, plants, and animals that may live in your house and neighborhood.

	NFI	3–6	I

Robbins, Ken. *A Flower Grows.* Dial, 1990.
1755 The author follows the transformation of an amaryllis bulb to an exquisite bloom with his time-lapse illustrations.

	NFI	K–3	I

Roberts, Willo Davis. *Sugar Isn't Everything: A Support Book, in Fiction Form, for the Young Diabetic.* Aladdin, 1988.
1756 Amy, an eleven-year-old girl, discovers she has diabetes. As this story unfolds, she learns about this disease and herself.

	F	6–9	

Robinson, Marlene M. *Who Knows This Nose?* Dodd, Mead, 1983.
1757 Photographs introduce each animal by its nose; then the animal's other characteristics are described.

	NFI	K–3	P

Rockwell, Anne. *My Spring Robin.* Macmillan, 1989.
1758 Through the observations of a small girl, the characteristics of spring are revealed.

	F	K–3	I

Rogers, Fred. *The New Baby.* Putnam, 1985.
1759 This book, which describes behaviors observed in an infant, appeals to the older child. Mr. Rogers also explains how a child's own emotions may enhance or detract from a positive interaction with a new sibling.

	NFN	K–6	P

Romanova, Natalia. *Once There Was a Tree.* Dial, 1989.
1760 The delicately detailed illustrations lend substance to this book from the Soviet Union, which describes the ecosystem in an old tree stump.

	F	K–6	I

Room for Me and a Mountain Lion: Poetry of Open Spaces. Selected by Nancy Farrick. M. Evans, 1989.
1761 This collection of over 100 poems that is divided into sections on mountains, woods, prairies, waves, ice, and open fields celebrates the beauty and wonder of the natural world.

	P	3–6	I

Rose, Kenneth J. *The Body in Time.* John Wiley, 1989.
1762 The author explores human biological processes in relation to the time it takes for these processes to take place.

	NFN	9–12	

	Type of literature	Grade span	Illustrations
Ryden, Hope. *America's Bald Eagle.* Putnam, 1985. **1763** The author describes the growth and development of young eagles and the environment that is critical for their survival. [Ecology]	NFI	3–9	P
Ryden, Hope. *Lily Pond: Four Years with a Family of Beavers.* William Morrow, 1989. **1764** The author uses vivid descriptions as she follows the daily life of a beaver family. [Ecology]	NFN	6–12	P
Ryden, Hope. *Wild Animals of Africa ABC.* Dutton, 1989. **1765** This alphabet book has color photographs of African animals in their natural habitats.	NFI	K–3	P
Ryder, Joanne. *Catching the Wind.* William Morrow, 1989. **1766** In this fantasy story a girl turns into a goose for one wonderful day, learning what it feels like to fly.	F	K–3	I
Ryder, Joanne. *Hello Tree!* Dutton, 1991. **1767** Bold illustrations and a poetic text describe the wonders of trees.	P	K–6	I
Ryder, Joanne. *Inside Turtle's Shell: And Other Poems of the Field.* Macmillan, 1985. **1768** Simple poems combine with delicate illustrations to describe events from the lives of the creatures who live in a small meadow and in a pond.	P	3–9	I
Ryder, Joanne. *Lizards in the Sun.* William Morrow, 1990. **1769** The author takes an imaginative look at the anole, the American chameleon. She describes its habitat and the changes that occur when it changes colors.	F	K–3	I
Ryder, Joanne. *Mockingbird Morning.* Four Winds, 1989. **1770** Paintings of a young girl taking a morning walk brighten this collection of poems about fields and woods.	F	3–6	I
Ryder, Joanne. *The Snail's Spell.* Viking, 1992. **1771** The author takes us into the world of a snail to observe its natural responses to its environment.	F	K–6	I
Ryder, Joanne. *Step into the Night.* Four Winds, 1988. **1772** The illustrations create a strong sense of night and shadows in this book about the sounds and movements of animals during the evening hours.	NFN	K–6	I
Ryder, Joanne. *Where Butterflies Grow.* Dutton, 1989. **1773** In this book, from a caterpillar's point of view, the author describes the chrysalis and the butterfly stages. She also suggests ways to encourage butterflies to live in your garden.	F	K–6	I
Ryder, Joanne. *White Bear, Ice Bear.* William Morrow, 1989. **1774** In this book a child imagines becoming an animal. The author describes how the bear looks, feels, and acts.	F	K–6	I
Rylant, Cynthia. *This Year's Garden.* Aladdin, 1987. **1775** The author introduces a country family that delights in the seasonal changes in their garden.	F	K–3	I

	Type of literature	Grade span	Illustrations
San Souci, Daniel. *North Country Nights.* Doubleday, 1990. **1776** This exquisite picture book re-creates a quiet, moonlit winter night in the forest. As the nocturnal animals come out to hunt, the author shows the predator-prey relationships.	F	K–3	I
Sattler, Helen Roney. *The Book of Eagles.* Lothrop, Lee and Shepard, 1989. **1777** This book includes in-depth information about the eagle's history, variety, physical characteristics, life cycle, habitats, behavior, mating, and the raising of its young.	NFI	3–9	I
Sattler, Helen Roney. *Tyrannosaurus Rex and Its Kin: The Mesozoic Monsters.* Lothrop, Lee and Shepard, 1989. **1778** The author relates information about dinosaurs that is based on fossils, footprints, and related artifacts.	NFI	3–6	I
Sattler, Helen Roney. *Whales, the Nomads of the Sea.* Lothrop, Lee and Shepard, 1987. **1779** This global introduction to whales covers their history, varieties, physical characteristics, diet, and environment. The author makes many comparisons to people, animals, and trucks.	NFI	3–9	I
Sayre, Anne. *Rosalind Franklin and DNA.* Norton, 1978. **1780** This biography of Rosalind Franklin discusses her research, scientific accomplishments, and contributions to the early research on DNA.	B	9–12	
Scheffer, Victor B. *The Year of the Whale.** Scribner's, 1969. **1781** The author chronicles 12 months in the life of a young sperm whale. He also includes background information about whales in general.	NFN	6–12	I
Schmitz, Siegfried. *Fish Calendar.* Silver Burdett, 1986. **1782** This global introduction to fish in general also includes information about garden ponds, aquariums, and fishing.	NFI	3–6	I
Schnieper, Claudia. *Amazing Spiders.* Carolrhoda, 1989. **1783** Marvelous color photographs introduce the physical characteristics of spiders, their web-building techniques, their methods of hunting, and the care of their young.	NFI	3–9	P
Schnieper, Claudia. *Lizards.* Carolrhoda, 1990. **1784** Remarkable photographs enhance descriptions of a number of species of European lizards and anoles that are both egg layers and live bearers.	NFI	3–9	P
Schnieper, Claudia. *On the Trail of the Fox.* Lerner, 1987. **1785** Color photographs follow a vixen and her pups as they grow and mature. The author incorporates information about their habitats, behaviors, physical characteristics, and life cycles.	NFI	3–9	P
Schwartz, David M. *The Hidden Life of the Pond.* Crown Publishers, 1988. **1786** This spectacular picture book introduces the creatures that live in a pond. In many cases, the parent and babies are shown together. Additional books to see in this series are *The Hidden Life of the Forest* and The *Hidden Life of the Meadow.* [Ecology]	NFI	K–6	P

	Type of literature	Grade span	Illus-trations
Scott, Jack Denton. *Swans.* Putnam, 1988. **1787** The history, physical characteristics, behaviors, habitats, and life cycles of seven species of swans are introduced and discussed in this book.	NFN	6–9	P
Selsam, Millicent E. *The Amazing Dandelion.* William Morrow, 1977. **1788** Photographs and text introduce the life cycle of this extremely hearty plant that is found everywhere and surprisingly also has nutritional value.	NFI	K–6	P
Selsam, Millicent E. *Backyard Insects.* Scholastic, 1981. **1789** Photographs let the reader see the variety of insects lurking in the trees and bushes outdoors. The author discusses the ways they protect themselves and use camouflage to escape from their enemies.	NFI	K–6	P
Selsam, Millicent E. *How to Be a Nature Detective.* Harper, 1966. **1790** This introduction to identifying animals and studying their behavior begins with pets and then moves outside to show how to learn about wild animals by observing the clues they leave behind.	NFN	K–3	I
Selsam, Millicent E. *Milkweed.* William Morrow, 1967. **1791** In this introduction to the common milkweed plant, its growth, development, and uses are explained.	NFI	3–6	I
Selsam, Millicent E. *Popcorn.* William Morrow, 1976. **1792** American popcorn is presented in this detailed book that covers popcorn's history, structure, and reproduction. Many detailed photographs highlight the text.	NFN	3–6	P
Selsam, Millicent E. *Strange Creatures That Really Lived.* Scholastic, 1989. **1793** The author describes the odd creatures that lived on earth millions of years ago. She also explains how scientists learned about these creatures.	NFI	K–6	I
Selsam, Millicent E. and Joyce Hunt. *Keep Looking!* Macmillan, 1989. **1794** This book introduces winter wildlife in snow country. The reader needs to look carefully to see all the hidden birds and animals in the illustrations.	NFI	K–3	I
Shapiro, Gilbert. *A Skeleton in the Darkroom: Stories of Serendipity in Science.* Harper, 1986. **1795** These are the stories of seven scientists who "found something valuable when they were looking for something else." These scientific adventures illustrate the luck, perseverance, and prepared minds that favor serendipity.	NFN	9–12	I
Sharp, Pat. *Brain Power: Secrets of a Winning Team.* Lothrop, Lee and Shepard, 1984. **1796** The author describes the ways the parts of the brain work together so the organism can function normally. The illustrations show how the brain is divided into many subparts and how each subpart works with other parts.	NFI	6–9	I
Shelley, Mary. *Frankenstein.* Bantam, 1981. **1797** Mary Shelley was eighteen years old when she wrote this novel about Victor Frankenstein, who created his notorious monster.	SF	9–12	

	Type of literature	Grade span	Illus-trations
Shepherd, Elizabeth. *No Bones: A Key to Bugs and Slugs, Worms and Ticks, Spiders and Centipedes, and Other Creepy Crawlies.* Macmillan, 1988. **1798** This is a simply written, dichotomous key to invertebrates.	NFI	3–9	I
Showers, Paul. *A Drop of Blood.* Harper, 1989. **1799** The author's discussion of blood includes its protective powers, types, cells, and means of replenishment. The bright illustrations clarify the concepts and show a simplified circulatory system.	NFI	3–9	I
Showers, Paul. *What Happens to a Hamburger.* Harper, 1985. **1800** The author clearly explains the human digestive process and includes easy-to-follow drawings.	NFI	3–6	I
Silberstein, Mark, and Eileen Campbell. *Elkhorn Slough.* Monterey Bay Aquarium, 1989. **1801** This book introduces the Monterey area's Elkhorn Slough and describes its origin and continued development. There are a number of aerial photographs and photographs of the plants and animals that inhabit the area.	NFI	3–9	P
Silverstein, Alvin, and Virginia Silverstein. *Nature's Living Lights: Fireflies and Other Bioluminescent Creatures.* Little, Brown, 1988. **1802** This is a fascinating look at the natural light production of insects, fish, and bacteria that use lights for both survival and courtship.	NFI	3–6	P
Silverstein, Alvin, and Virginia B. Silverstein. *The Story of Your Foot.* Putnam, 1987. **1803** Scientific drawings expand this comprehensive discussion of the human foot.	NFI	6–9	S
Simon, Seymour. *The Secret Clocks: Time Senses of Living Things.* Viking, 1979. **1804** The internal "clocks" of fish, bees, birds, plants, and animals are introduced. Research through the years is described. The author includes suggestions for hands-on projects and experiments.	NFI	3–9	
Simon, Seymour. *Whales.* Harper, 1990. **1805** Whales are defined as sea mammals that breathe air. Both text and pictures describe their physical characteristics and their environment.	NFI	3–6	P
Singer, Marilyn. *Turtle in July.* Macmillan, 1989. **1806** Watercolor illustrations enhance this simple story that tells about the activities of a turtle during July.	P	K–6	I
Smith, Anthony. *The Body.* Walker and Company, 1968. **1807** The author presents fascinating information about a wide range of topics related to the human body.	NFI	6–12	
Smith, Trevor. *Amazing Lizards.* Knopf, 1991. **1808** Interesting information and marvelous photographs highlight a variety of unusual lizards.	NFI	3–6	I
Somme, Lauritz, and Sybille Kalas. *The Penguin Family Book.* Picture Book Studio, 1988. **1809** The penguins on Bouvet Island, in the Antarctic Ocean, are introduced in this book.	NFN	K–6	P

	Type of literature	Grade span	Illus-trations
Speare, Elizabeth George. *The Sign of the Beaver.* Dell, 1984. **1810** In this survival story set in colonial times, Matt, whose family has recently moved to the Maine wilderness, is befriended by an Indian boy who shares his knowledge of wilderness skills. Matt learns these skills and also learns to value and respect the Indians' ways. [Ecology]	F	3–9	
Stap, Don. *A Parrot Without a Name: The Search for the Last Unknown Birds on Earth.* University of Texas, 1991. **1811** The author describes an expedition into the Amazon basin specifically undertaken to discover, collect, and classify new species of birds.	NFI	9–12	P
Stewart, George. *Earth Abides.* Archive, 1976. **1812** In this science fiction tale, a small band of survivors struggles to keep civilization alive after a plague decimates the earth's human population. [Ecology]	SF	9–12	
Stolz, Mary. *Night of Ghosts and Hermits: Nocturnal Life on the Seashore.* Harcourt Brace Jovanovich, 1985. **1813** This book describes the small creatures that come out after dark to search for new homes, food, and a safe place to lay eggs.	NFN	3–9	I
Stone, Lynne. *Birds of Prey.* Children's Press, 1983. **1814** Birds of prey are introduced, defined, and examined in this book.	NFI	K–6	P
Strieber, Whitley. *Wolf of Shadows.* Fawcett, 1986. **1815** In this science fiction tale, an intelligent wolf joins a young woman and her child in an attempt to survive after a devastating nuclear war. [Ecology]	SF	6–12	
Strum, Shirley C. *Almost Human: A Journey into the World of Baboons.* Random House, 1987. **1816** This novel about baboons' behavior is based on the author's field research experiences.	NFN	9–12	
Sturgeon, Theodore. *More Than Human.* Ballantine, 1985. **1817** In this science fiction tale, several misfit children come together to form a new "gestalt" that is based on their parapsychological abilities.	SF	9–12	
Sussman, Susan, and Robert James. *Big Friend, Little Friend: A Book About Symbiosis.* Houghton Mifflin, 1989. **1818** Wonderful pictures introduce 14 sets of unusual animal friends that benefit from symbiosis.	NFI	3–9	P
Sussman, Susan, and Robert James. *Lies (People Believe) About Animals.* Whitman, 1987. **1819** The authors present fascinating facts about animals and the myths that people believe about them.	NFI	3–6	P
Tepper, Sheri S. *Grass.* Bantam, 1990. **1820** In this science fiction tale, the only place untouched by the plague is a world called Grass. Viruses, mutations, and the will to survive are the elements of this densely plotted story. [Ecology]	SF	9–12	

	Type of literature	Grade span	Illus- trations

Thomas, Lewis. *The Lives of a Cell: Notes of a Biology Watcher.* Bantam, 1984.

1821 These essays, which include biological and philosophical topics, capture the wonder felt by individuals associated with the sciences.

| | NFN | 6–12 | |

Thomas, Lewis. *The Medusa and the Snail: More Notes of a Biology Watcher.* Bantam, 1979.

1822 The author writes about a rich diversity of topics with warmth and charm.

| | NFI | 9–12 | |

Thomas, Lewis. *The Youngest Science: Notes of a Medicine Watcher.* Penguin, 1983.

1823 A physician's son reflects on medicine's evolution from an art to high-powered research.

| | B | 9–12 | |

Titherington, Jeanne. *Pumpkin, Pumpkin.* William Morrow, 1990.

1824 In this picture book Jamie plants a pumpkin seed, watches the pumpkin grow, and then uses it for Halloween.

| | F | K–3 | I |

Todd, Frank. *The Sea World Book of Penguins.* Harcourt Brace Jovanovich, 1984.

1825 This is the definitive book on penguins. Information is included about their adaptation to aquatic habitats, their physical characteristics, their status in the wild, and the special problems involved in maintaining penguins in zoos. Beautiful photographs of wild penguins accompany the text.

| | NFI | 3–6 | P |

Tokuda, Wendy, and Richard Hall. *Humphrey, The Lost Whale.* Heian, 1989.

1826 This is an account of the humpback whale who was lost in San Francisco Bay and the Sacramento Delta's waters. The author describes the successful efforts to return Humphrey to the Pacific Ocean.

| | NFN | K–3 | I |

Toye, William. *The Loon's Necklace.* Oxford, 1977.

1827 The author retells the Tsimshian Indian legend that describes the origins of the loon's markings. [Folklore]

| | NFN | K–3 | I |

Turner, Ann. *Heron Street.* Harper, 1989.

1828 This is the story of what happened when people began to build near a marsh where herons, ducks, geese, and raccoons lived. The story continues to describe Heron Street today, with the automobiles chugging down the streets and the animals gone.

| | NFN | K–6 | I |

Tuttle, Merlin D. *America's Neighborhood Bats: Understanding and Learning to Live in Harmony with Them.* University of Texas, 1988.

1829 Bats and misconceptions about them are discussed in this book that includes information about their behaviors, feeding habits, and diseases. Beautiful photographs accompany the text.

| | NFI | 9–12 | P |

Udry, Janice May. *A Tree Is Nice.* Harper, 1987.

1830 Trees are described as nice for a variety of important events in our daily lives.

| | NFN | K–3 | I |

	Type of literature	Grade span	Illustrations
Van Soelen, Philip. *Cricket in the Grass: And Other Stories.* Scribner's, 1979. **1831** The reader is invited to enter a variety of ecosystems and through careful observations learn about their life cycles and food chains. [Ecology]	NFI	6–9	S
Vassilissa. *Kiou the Owl.* Bedrick, 1984. **1832** Kiou the owl is hatched, grows up, learns to fly and hunt, and establishes his own home in this tale. [Ecology]	NFN	K–6	I
Vinge, Joan D. *Psion.* Dell, 1990. **1833** In this science fiction novel, a child from the slums agrees to use his telepathic powers to help the government fight evil.	SF	6–9	I
Vogel, Carole, and Kathryn Goldiner. *The Great Yellowstone Fire.* Little, Brown, 1990. **1834** Pictures and text introduce Yellowstone National Park, the fire of 1988, and its effects on the ecology.	NFI	3–9	P
The Voyage of the Mimi. Edited by Lorin Driggs. Holt, Rinehart and Winston, 1985. **1835** This is the story of the *Mimi*, the ship that scientists chartered to study humpback whales. The book describes the people involved and has a number of interesting activities.	NFN	3–9	P
Wakefield, Pat, and Larry Carrara. *A Moose for Jessica.* Dutton, 1987. **1836** The Vermont bull moose who fell in love with a Hereford cow is the focus of this true story that made headlines. Color photographs accompany the text.	NFN	3–9	P
Walters, Mark Jerome. *The Dance of Life: Courtship in the Animal Kingdom.* William Morrow, 1988. **1837** The author describes elaborate animal courtship and mating rituals. He starts with small fish and continues to primates, specifically pygmy chimpanzees.	NFN	9–12	P
Watson, James D. *The Double Helix.* Atheneum, 1990. **1838** This is Watson's personal account of his collaboration with other scientists in the discovery of the DNA molecule.	NFN	9–12	
Watts, Barrie. *Bird's Nest.* Silver Burdett, 1987. **1839** Birds' nests are introduced in this book, with details of their construction and uses.	NFI	K–6	P
Watts, Barrie. *Butterfly and Caterpillar.* Silver Burdett, 1989. **1840** The life cycle of a butterfly is this book's subject, with superb, enlarged, color photographs that depict mating, egg laying, and a caterpillar hatching and growing.	NFI	K–3	P
Watts, Barrie. *Dandelion.* Silver Burdett, 1987. **1841** One of North America's most familiar flowers, the dandelion is described in its complete life cycle.	NFI	K–3	P
Watts, Barrie. *Hamster.* Silver Burdett, 1989. **1842** Wonderful pictures enhance a text that covers baby hamsters' growth until they are ready to leave the nest.	NFI	K–3	P

	Type of literature	Grade span	Illus-trations
Watts, Barrie. *Mushroom.* Silver Burdett, 1986. **1843** The growth of mushrooms is described and illustrated with both photographs and line drawings. Details reveal all the mystery of this fungal growth.	NFI	K–3	P
Watts, Barrie. *Tomato.* Silver Burdett, 1990. **1844** Crisp, color photographs enhance the basic information on the growth and development of tomatoes.	NFI	K–3	P
Weaver, Harriett E. *Frosty: A Raccoon to Remember.* PB, 1986. **1845** California's first female state park ranger tells the story of an orphaned raccoon that was rescued, bottle-fed, and returned to the wild.	NFN	6–12	
Weissmann, Gerald. *They All Laughed at Christopher Columbus: Tales of Medicine and the Art of Discovery.* Random, 1987. **1846** The author looks at the creative processes involved in medical discoveries.	NFN	6–12	
Wertheim, Anne. *The Intertidal Wilderness.* Sierra, 1985. **1847** This book presents a photographic trip through rocky shore tide pools. The text emphasizes the diversity of plant and animal life and the relationships between these organisms and their environment.	NFI	6–12	P
Westberg-Peters, Lisa. *The Condor.* Macmillan, 1990. **1848** Many beautiful photographs illustrate the story of the condor's battle with extinction.	NFI	3–6	P
Wiewandt, Thomas. *The Hidden Life of the Desert.* Crown Publishers, 1990. **1849** The interdependence of life in the desert is detailed in this book, which shows how many unusual plants and animals have learned to live in this harsh ecosystem. Numerous color photographs accompany the text.	NFI	3–6	P
Wildsmith, Brian. *Squirrels.* Oxford, 1987. **1850** This delightful picture book introduces the special adaptations and behaviors of squirrels.	F	K–3	I
Wilkins, Malcolm. *Plantwatching: How Plants Remember, Tell Time, Form Partnerships and More.* Facts on File, 1988. **1851** This is a detailed examination of plants, plant organs, tissues, and plant cells through descriptions, photographs, microphotographs, and electron microphotographs. The author covers circadian behavior, physiological processes, and symbiotic relationships.	NFI	9–12	P
Wilson, Dorothy Clarke. *I Will Be a Doctor! The Story of America's First Woman Physician.* Abingdon, 1983. **1852** Elizabeth Blackwell's childhood, education, and prominence as a physician, educator, and social worker are described in this fictionalized biography.	B	6–9	
Wren, M. K. *A Gift upon the Shore.* Ballantine, 1991. **1853** Two women struggle to stay alive and to preserve their civilization during the nuclear winter and its aftermath.	SF	9–12	

	Type of literature	Grade span	Illustrations
Wyndham, John. *Day of the Triffids.* Ballantine, 1985.	SF	9–12	
Wyndham, John. *The Midwich Cuckoos.* Ballantine, 1957.	SF	9–12	
Yolen, Jane. *Owl Moon.* Putnam, 1987.	F	K–6	I
Yoshida, Toshi. *Elephant Crossing.* Putnam, 1989.	NFN	K–6	I
Yoshida, Toshi. *Young Lions.* Putnam, 1989.	NFN	K–6	I
Yue, Charlotte, and David Yue. *The Igloo.* Houghton Mifflin, 1988.	NFN	6–9	I

Wyndham, John. *Day of the Triffids.* Ballantine, 1985.
1854 In this science fiction tale, the Triffids begin as harmless plants. However, human error turns them into semisentient flora that threaten to take over the earth.

Wyndham, John. *The Midwich Cuckoos.* Ballantine, 1957.
1855 Superchildren with great *psi* powers are born in the English village of Midwich in this science fiction tale. These children are perceived as a threat that must be destroyed.

Yolen, Jane. *Owl Moon.* Putnam, 1987.
1856 In this gentle, poetic story, a little girl goes owling with her father for the first time on a cold winter's night. They enjoy a special feeling for each other and for nature. [Ecology]

Yoshida, Toshi. *Elephant Crossing.* Putnam, 1989.
1857 In this story, the leader of a herd of African elephants remembers a time when even their great size and strength could not protect the elephants against the swarms of grasshoppers.

Yoshida, Toshi. *Young Lions.* Putnam, 1989.
1858 In this story three young lions leave the safety of the pride to go on their first hunt. It is a grand adventure as they cross the plain, coming into contact with the great variety of animals.

Yue, Charlotte, and David Yue. *The Igloo.* Houghton Mifflin, 1988.
1859 The arctic way of life is described in this book that discusses the peoples who live in this harsh environment, the construction of their igloos, and their need for special clothing.

MATHEMATICS

2+2=4

The power and beauty of mathematics, which pervades all human endeavors, are illustrated in the broad spectrum of literature included in this section. Many books, such as Laurie Buxton's *Mathematics for Everyone*, Petr Beckmann's *A History of Pi*, and Douglas Hofstadter's *Gödel, Escher and Bach*, chronicle the history as well as the applications of mathematical thought. Counting books like *Anno's Counting House*, by Matsumasa Anno, and Donald Crews's *Ten Black Dots* involve young children with numbers in a variety of delightful and creative contexts. Books such as Eric Laithwaite's *Size: The Measure of Things* and Manfred Riedel's *Winning with Numbers* help make mathematical ideas comprehensible. Recreational mathematics is the focus of *Mathematics, Magic, and Mystery,* by Martin Gardner. Other books go far beyond the domain of mathematics alone. Mathematical ideas are integrally woven into the literary classics of *Gulliver's Travels,* by Jonathan Swift, *Alice in Wonderland,* by Lewis Carroll, and *The Adventures of Sherlock Holmes,* by Arthur Conan Doyle. The uses of mathematics in other cultures are shared in books such as *Grandfather Tang's Story,* by Ann Tompert. *The Golden Mean,* by Charles Linn, and *Math Talk: Mathematical Ideas in Poems for Two Voices,* by Theoni Pappas, illustrate the relationship of mathematics to the fine arts.

	Type of literature	Grade span	Illustrations
Abbott, Edwin. *Flatland: A Romance of Many Dimensions.* Viking, 1987. **1860** This classic tale about life in a two-dimensional world describes a pecking order based on shape. Part of the author's purpose was to satirize social issues of his Victorian era.	SF	6–12	
Adams, Pam. *There Were Ten in the Bed.* Child's Play, 1979. **1861** This delightful song has been illustrated and made into a book with a turning dial that causes the ten multicultural children to fall out of bed one at a time.	F	K–3	I
Adler, David. *Roman Numerals.* Harper, 1977. **1862** This book introduces the number systems from several ancient cultures and specifically shows how to add and subtract with Roman numerals.	NFI	3–6	I
Adler, David. *Three-D, Two-D, One-D.* Harper, 1974. **1863** The author defines and explains the concept of *dimension*, using everyday objects as examples.	NFI	3–6	I
Adler, Irving. *Mathematics.* Doubleday, 1990. **1864** The relationships between mathematics and nature, art, and music are highlighted in this book. The author discusses the large part mathematics plays in daily life and introduces odd-even numbers, angles, square roots, polygons, and computer activities.	NFI	3–6	I
Aker, Suzanne. *What Comes in Two's, Three's, and Four's?* Simon and Schuster, 1990. **1865** This introduction to numbers and dimensions uses as examples everyday patterns that children can see all around them.	F	K–3	I
Albers, Donald J., and G. L. Alexanderson. *Mathematical People: Profiles and Interviews.* Contemporary Books, 1986. **1866** Numerous photographs accompany these interviews and profiles, which provide insight into the philosophies and mathematical work of 26 eminent mathematicians.	B	6–12	P

	Type of literature	Grade span	Illustrations
Allen, Pamela. *A Lion in the Night.* Putnam, 1986. **1867** Spatial concepts and mapping are introduced in this simple adventure story about a lion.	F	3–6	I
Allen, Pamela. *Mr. Archimedes' Bath.* Harper, n.d. **1868** Mr. Archimedes solves his problem of an overflowing bathtub and introduces concepts of volume and displacement.	F	3–6	I
Allen, Pamela. *Who Sank the Boat?* Putnam, 1990. **1869** In a rhyming story about five friends who go sailing, the author introduces concepts of order, capacity, mass, balance, and problem solving.	F	3–6	I
Anno, Mitsumasa. *Anno's Counting Book.* Harper, 1986. **1870** This picture book starts with a blank landscape for zero and adds 12 seasonal landscape features.	NFI	K–3	I
Anno, Mitsumasa. *Anno's Counting House.* Putnam, 1982. **1871** Ten children can be counted through cutout windows as they move from one house to another.	NFI	K–3	I
Anno, Mitsumasa. *Anno's Math Games.* Putnam, 1987. **1872** The games in this collection progress from easy to quite complex.	NFN	3–9	I
Anno, Mitsumasa. *Anno's Math Games II.* Putnam, 1989. **1873** Picture puzzles and games introduce mathematical principles, concepts, theories of sequence, measurement, ordinal numbers, and direction.	NFN	3–9	I
Anno, Mitsumasa. *Anno's Math Games III.* Putnam, 1991. **1874** Picture puzzles and the idea of a magic liquid that stretches or shrinks introduce complicated mathematical concepts, abstract thinking, geometry and topology, and make them fun.	NFN	3–9	I
Anno, Mitsumasa. *Anno's Mysterious Multiplying Jar.* Putnam, 1983. **1875** The contents of a Japanese jar, colorfully illustrated, are used to introduce the concept of numerical patterns and linear multiplication. The afterword contains information on factorials.	NFN	3–9	I
Anno, Mitsumasa. *Topsy-Turvies: More Pictures to Stretch the Imagination.* Philomel, 1989. **1876** This picture book has lots of optical illusions that stretch reality with their bends and changes. The mathematical focus is on the variety of spatial and geometric possibilities.	NFI	3–9	I
Anno, Mitsumasa. *Topsy-Turvies: Pictures to Stretch the Imagination.* Weatherhill, 1970. **1877** In this picture book there are plenty of opportunities to find interesting "impossibilities" in perspective and gravity.	NFI	3–9	I
Anno, Mitsumasa. *Upside Downers: Pictures to Stretch the Imagination.* Putnam, 1988. **1878** This book introduces and explores point of view, reverse images, optics, and logic in a fanciful Land of Cards.	F	3–6	I
Ardley, Neil. *Making Metric Measurements.* Franklin Watts, 1984. **1879** This book introduces a variety of metric experiments to calculate weight, size, speed, height, and volume.	NFI	6–9	P

	Type of literature	Grade span	Illus-trations
Argent, Kerry, and Rod Trinca. *One Woolly Wombat.* Kane Miller, 1985. **1880** Alliterations and rhymes make this counting book with an Australian setting fun for children of any age.	F	K–3	I
Ashabranner, Melissa, and Brent Ashabranner. *Counting America: The Story of the United States Census.* Putnam, 1989. **1881** The United States census is introduced with information about its history, the arduous task of conducting a census, and the importance of the data collected.	NFI	6–9	P
Bang, Molly. *Ten, Nine, Eight.* William Morrow, 1991. **1882** This introduction to both prediction and counting patterns uses the familiar bedtime countdown as the story's focus.	F	K–3	I
Base, Graeme. *The Eleventh Hour: A Curious Mystery.* Harry Abrams, 1990. **1883** Problem solving and skill development abound in this mystery story that has colorful, complex illustrations. The answer is sealed in a page at the end of the book.	F	3–9	I
Becker, John. *Seven Little Rabbits.* Scholastic, 1985. **1884** In this counting story seven little rabbits go walking down the road to call on toad, but, one by one, they tire and fall asleep. The rhythmic language makes the tale delightful to read.	NFN	K–3	I
Beckmann, Petr. *A History of Pi.* Golem, 1971. **1885** This book traces the history of *pi* as a mirror to the history of man.	NFN	9–12	
Bendick, Jeanne. *How Much and How Many: The Story of Weights and Measures.* Franklin Watts, 1989. **1886** The history of measurement is discussed from ancient times to the present and our modern technology. Both standard and nonstandard measures are discussed.	NFI	6–12	
Bendick, Jeanne, and Marcia Levin. *Take a Number.* McGraw-Hill, 1961. **1887** The author explores the development of number systems and how we have organized them in newer and more usable ways.	NFI	3–6	I
Bishop, Owen. *Yardsticks of the Universe.* Bedrick, 1982. **1888** The author's goal is to show that the ability to measure is essential to scientific discoveries. The methods for measuring physical quantities, such as the mass of the earth, the speed of light, the mass of an electron, and the distance to astronomical objects, are illustrated with clear diagrams.	NFI	6–9	I
Blegvad, Lenore. *One Is for the Sun.* Harcourt Brace Jovanovich, 1968. **1889** The rhymed text counts to ten and then to ten million using sights and sounds familiar to a child.	F	K–3	I
Blocksma, Mary. *Reading the Numbers: A Survival Guide to the Measurements, Numbers, and Sizes Encountered in Everyday Life.* Viking, 1989. **1890** This book is organized alphabetically; however, the topics are de-scribed and explained in relation to their numbers.	NFI	K–3	I

	Type of literature	Grade span	Illus-trations

Boynton, Sandra. *Hippos Go Berserk.* Little, Brown, 1977.

1891 A lonesome hippo calls all his friends, inviting them to a party. The mathematical focus is on counting forward and backward as the friends arrive for the party and then leave.

F K–3 I

Branley, Franklyn M. *Think Metric!* Harper, 1972.

1892 In an amusing but straightforward way, the author helps readers discover the advantages of the metric system to solve problems.

NFI 6–9

Briggs, Raymond. *Jim and the Beanstalk.* Putnam, 1989.

1893 In this updated folktale, Jim revisits the giant's house and uses measurements to interest and help him.

F 3–6 I

Bunting, Eve. *How Many Days to America? A Thanksgiving Story.* Houghton Mifflin, 1990.

1894 A family's travels to the United States provide the context for an understanding of counting, calendars, and the relativity of time.

F 3–6 I

Burger, Dionys. *Sphereland.* Harper, 1983.

1895 This sequel to Edwin Abbott's *Flatland* is an enjoyable story that weaves together non-Euclidean geometry, curved space, and other dimensional realities into a fantasyland.

F 6–12

Burningham, John. *The Shopping Basket.* Harper, 1980.

1896 Counting, subtraction, patterns, sequencing, triangular numbers, location, and mapping come into play when Stephen's shopping trip turns into a fantastic series of adventures.

F 3–6 I

Burns, Marilyn. *Math for Smarty Pants.* Little, Brown, 1982.

1897 Opportunities are suggested for experimenting with numbers, shapes, strategy games, and other problem-solving techniques in this captivating book.

NFI 3–9 I

Buxton, Laurie. *Mathematics for Everyone.* Schocken, 1986.

1898 In this day of calculators and computers, the author offers fascinating insights into everyday mathematics. She discusses strands in depth and illustrates the purpose and need for calculus.

NFI 9–12 I

Carle, Eric. *One, Two, Three to the Zoo.* Putnam, 1990.

1899 In this colorful picture book, readers count up to ten zoo animals riding on a train.

F K–3 I

Carle, Eric. *The Secret Birthday Message.* Harper, 1986.

1900 The math focus is simple geometry and shapes. The pages are cutouts that match the shapes of the messages Tim is given as he searches for his present.

F K–3 I

Carle, Eric. *The Very Busy Spider.* Putnam, 1989.

1901 The spider spinning a web does not allow anyone to stop the work before it is completed in this simple story. The mathematics focus is on spatial and textural patterns.

F K–3 I

Carle, Eric. *The Very Hungry Caterpillar.* Putnam, 1989.

1902 This fanciful picture book exaggerates the number and variety of foods a caterpillar eats as it introduces amounts, estimates, numbers, counting, days, and fractions.

F K–3 I

	Type of literature	Grade span	Illustrations
Carroll, Lewis. *Alice in Wonderland.* Scholastic, 1985. **1903** Lewis Carroll, who in real life was mathematics professor Charles L. Dodgson, writes about a little girl who falls down a rabbit hole and discovers a world of nonsensical and amusing characters. Carroll plays with conventional notions of logic, time, and dimension to create this much-loved story.	F	6–12	I
Carroll, Susan. *How Big Is a Brachiosaurus? Fascinating Facts About Dinosaurs.* Putnam, 1986. **1904** The author presents information about dinosaurs that allows their comparison to each other, buildings, and common animals.	NFN	K–3	I
Chapman, Steven. *How Many? How Much?* Follett, 1972. **1905** A boy discovers many interesting mathematical problems and puzzles as he rides his bike. The solutions are accurate and, sometimes, silly, depending on the questions.	F	3–6	I
Cleveland, David. *The April Rabbits.* Scholastic, 1988. **1906** This book can be used for counting, introducing the months, or just for fun. On April 1 rabbits enter Robert's life and participate in a variety of interesting activities. At the end of April, they disappear.	F	K–3	I
Crews, Donald. *Bicycle Race.* Greenwillow, 1985. **1907** A colorful bicycle race provides an opportunity to discuss the positions of numbers and ordinal numbers.	F	K–3	I
Crews, Donald. *Ten Black Dots.* Greenwillow, 1986. **1908** This book very creatively describes the variety of ways that ten black dots can be used.	F	K–3	I
Demi. *Demi's Count the Animals One-Two-Three.* Putnam, 1990. **1909** Cheerful illustrations and bright poetry attract children to the many creatures depicted and then encourage children to count them.	F	K–3	I
Dennis, J. Richard. *Fractions Are Parts of Things.* Crowell, 1971. **1910** The geometric figures and fractions are colorfully illustrated, helping to make the explanations simple and the applications clear.	NFI	K–3	I
Digital Deli: The Lunch Group. Edited by Steve Ditlea. Workman, 1984. **1911** This wide-ranging collection of articles on computers touches on their history, their impact on society, and their applications. The insights are surprisingly fresh, despite the technological advances that date some articles.	NFI	9–12	
D'Ignazio, Fred, and Allen L. Wold. *The Science of Artificial Intelligence.* Franklin Watts, 1988. **1912** This book defines artificial intelligence and how it applies to computer technology. The author also discusses the limits of artificial intelligence compared to the human brain. [Technology]	NFI	6–12	P
Doyle, Arthur Conan. *The Adventures of Sherlock Holmes.* Berkley, 1985. **1913** Using logic to solve problems and mysteries is stressed in this classic collection of short stories.	F	6–12	
Dunham, Meredith. *Numbers: How Do You Say It?* Lothrop, Lee and Shepard, 1987. **1914** Counting is introduced in four languages.	NFI	K–6	I

	Type of literature	Grade span	Illus-trations
Dunham, Meredith. *Shapes: How Do You Say It?* Lothrop, Lee and Shepard, 1987.	NFI	K–6	I
1915 Shapes are introduced in four languages, through bold illustrations in bright colors.			
Dunrea, Olivier. *Deep Down Underground.* Macmillan, 1989.	NFN	K–3	I
1916 Rhymes and clever illustrations make counting these underground creatures lots of fun.			
Eichenberg, Fritz. *Dancing in the Moon: Counting Rhymes.* Harcourt Brace Jovanovich, 1975.	F	K–3	I
1917 Catchy rhymes and animal illustrations help young children learn to count to 20.			
Emberley, Barbara. *Drummer Hoff.* Simon and Schuster, 1985.	F	K–3	I
1918 Math concepts are introduced with bright, bold illustrations and repetitive, rhyming language that describes the firing of a cannon.			
Ernst, Lisa Campbell. *Up to Ten and Down Again.* Lothrop, Lee and Shepard, 1986.	F	K–3	I
1919 In this counting book, children arrive for a picnic in the park and then leave when it starts to rain.			
Feelings, Muriel. *Moja Means One.* Dial, 1976.	NFI	K–6	I
1920 This counting book encourages counting from one to ten in Swahili.			
Ferris, Jeri. *What Are You Figuring Now? A Story About Benjamin Banneker.* Carolrhoda, 1988.	B	6–9	I
1921 This biography introduces the colonial Afro-American farmer Benjamin Banneker, who was a self-taught astronomer, surveyor, and mathematician.			
Fisher, Leonard Everett. *Calendar Art: Thirteen Days, Weeks, Months, and Years from Around the World.* Macmillan, 1987.	NFI	3–9	I
1922 Calendars from ancient civilizations are introduced with descriptions of each civilization's need to measure time and its attempts to meet this need.			
Fisher, Leonard Everett. *Number Art: Thirteen 1, 2, 3's from Around the World.* Macmillan, 1984.	NFI	3–9	I
1923 The number systems of 13 ancient cultures are introduced and depicted in this book.			
Freeman, Mae. *Finding Out About Shapes.* McGraw Hill, 1969.	NFI	K–6	I
1924 This book encourages higher level thinking as shapes are discovered, compared, felt, used, and rearranged.			
Froman, Robert. *Angles Are Easy as Pie.* Harper, 1976.	NFI	3–6	I
1925 The engaging text and illustrations enhance the differences between big and small angles and illustrate how they can form triangles. The book also explores ways people in different professions use angles.			
Froman, Robert. *The Greatest Guessing Game: A Book About Dividing.* Crowell, 1978.	NFI	3–6	I
1926 The concept of division is reinforced through the fun of this "guessing" game. Surprisingly, this is a trial-and-error plan that keeps young readers interested and allays their fear of division problems.			

	Type of literature	Grade span	Illus-trations
Froman, Robert. *Less Than Nothing Is Really Something.* Crowell, 1973.	NFI	3–6	I
1927 Clever illustrations introduce negative numbers, their relationships to positive numbers, and the important uses for negative numbers.			
Gackenbach, Dick. *A Bag Full of Pups.* Ticknor and Fields, 1983.	F	3–6	I
1928 The mathematical focus is on counting, subtraction, and equations as Mr. Mullins finds new homes for the 12 pups.			
Gag, Wanda. *Millions of Cats.* Putnam, 1977.	F	K–3	I
1929 Focusing on very large numbers, this story is about an elderly couple who look at great numbers of cats before finding their kitten.			
Gardner, Beau. *Can You Imagine? A Counting Book.* Putnam, 1987.	F	K–3	I
1930 This counting book incorporates rhymes as the count goes up to 12.			
Gardner, Martin. *Mathematics, Magic, and Mystery.* Dover, 1956.	NFI	9–12	I
1931 Mathematical puzzles—with the appearance of magic and mystery—demonstrate probability, sets, the theory of numbers, and topology and make them fun.			
Gibbons, Gail. *Willy and His Wheel Wagon.* Prentice Hall, 1975.	F	K–3	I
1932 Willie adds the numbers of wheels to be serviced as he repairs bikes, carts, and wagons.			
Giganti, Paul, Jr. *How Many Snails?* Greenwillow, 1988.	F	K–3	I
1933 Interesting walks form the backdrop for an introduction to the concept of sets. In this unusual counting book, young readers are encouraged to observe and count the interesting things along the way.			
Gillings, Richard. *Mathematics in the Time of the Pharaohs.* Dover, 1982.	NFI	9–12	I
1934 This scholarly book examines the development of Egyptian mathematics, from its origins in practical and commercial computations to its applications involving direct and inverse proportions, linear equations, and trigonometric functions.			
Gleick, James. *Chaos: Making a New Science.* Viking, 1988.	NFN	9–12	
1935 The author explores the new area of science and mathematics based on nonlinear phenomena. This book is challenging reading.			
Grifalconi, Ann. *The Village of Round and Square Houses.* Little, Brown, 1986.	F	3–9	I
1936 This African tale, which explains why the men live in square houses and the women live in round ones, is an excellent introduction to early geometry.			
Hellen, Nancy. *The Bus Stop.* Orchard Books, 1991.	F	K–3	I
1937 People are arranged in order (ordinal numbers) while waiting for the bus and while in the bus. The short pages and the page cutouts help to make this clever counting book fascinating and fun.			
Hoban, Tana. *Circles, Triangles, and Squares.* Macmillan, 1974.	NFI	K–6	P
1938 Pictures of artifacts that form circles, triangles, and squares introduce simple geometry.			

	Type of literature	Grade span	Illus-trations
Hoban, Tana. *Count and See.* Macmillan, 1972. **1939** This counting book includes familiar items, Arabic numbers, and dots to teach counting sequentially up to 15.	NFI	K–6	P
Hoban, Tana. *Over, Under, and Through: And Other Spatial Concepts.* Macmillan, 1987. **1940** Pictures illustrate and encourage understanding of spatial concepts.	F	K–6	P
Hoban, Tana. *Round and Round and Round.* Greenwillow, 1983. **1941** The color photographs depict the great variety of round objects we see frequently.	NFI	K–6	P
Hoban, Tana. *Shapes and Things.* Macmillan, 1970. **1942** The photographs show a variety of the geometric shapes in our world.	NFI	K–6	P
Hoban, Tana. *Shapes, Shapes, Shapes.* Greenwillow, 1986. **1943** This picture book of photographs depicts everyday objects of a variety of geometric shapes.	NFI	K–6	P
Hoban, Tana. *Take Another Look.* Greenwillow, 1981. **1944** This wordless picture book encourages observational skills and problem solving with comparisons of natural and manufactured items. Certain pages focus attention on the solving of intriguing mysteries.	NFI	K–6	P
Hoban, Tana. *Twenty-six Letters and Ninety-nine Cents.* Greenwillow, 1987. **1945** This interesting picture book can be read front to back and from back to front. In one direction, coins introduce counting; in the other, common items introduce the alphabet. This is a very visual book, with bright primary colors and crisp pictures.	NFI	K–6	P
Hoffman, Paul. *Archimedes' Revenge.* Fawcett, 1989. **1946** The author samples a fascinating array of problems in all fields of mathematics and gives a picture of both pure and applied mathematics.	NFN	9–12	
Hofstadter, Douglas. *Gödel, Escher, Bach: An Eternal Golden Braid.* Random House, 1989. **1947** This challenging and lengthy book discusses the continuity of thought in Bach's music, Escher's drawings, and Gödel's theorem of logic. The notion of artificial intelligence is also discussed.	NFN	9–12	
Hooper, Meredith. *Seven Eggs.* Harper, 1986. **1948** In this alluring book, a different bird or reptile hatches from an egg on each day of the week.	F	K–3	I
Hughes, Shirley. *When We Went to the Park.* Lothrop, Lee and Shepard, 1985. **1949** The focus is on counting and sequencing as a little girl tells about everything she sees and counts at the park.	F	K–3	I
Humphrey, Henry, and Deirdre O'Meara-Humphrey. *When Is Now?* Doubleday, 1980. **1950** Calendars and other time divisions are explained in great detail in this book, which includes models of ancient timekeeping devices and the directions for making them.	NFI	6–12	S

	Type of literature	Grade span	Illustrations
Huntley, H. E. *Divine Proportion: A Study in Mathematical Beauty.* Dover, 1970. **1951** According to Poincaré, quoted in this book: "The mathematician does not study pure mathematics because it is useful; he studies it because he delights in it and he delights in it because it is beautiful." Careful attention rewards the reader with an appreciation of the power, grace, and beauty of a variety of mathematical topics.	NFN	6–12	
Hutchins, Pat. *Changes, Changes.* Aladdin, 1987. **1952** This picture book introduces and explores geometric and spatial relations and sequencing as a couple, made of wood, rearrange a set of blocks as their daily needs change.	F	K–3	I
Hutchins, Pat. *Clocks and More Clocks.** Macmillan, 1970. **1953** In this humorous tale, Mr. Higgins knows clocks are a useful tool for telling time, but he has not quite grasped the notion of the passage of time.	F	K–3	I
Hutchins, Pat. *The Doorbell Rang.* William Morrow, 1989. **1954** More and more friends arrive and are invited to share a plate of cookies, illustrating the mathematical processes of division and multiplication.	F	K–3	I
Hutchins, Pat. *One Hunter.* Greenwillow, 1982. **1955** In this humorous counting book, an old hunter is oblivious to the jungle animals around him.	F	K–3	I
Johnston, Tony. *Whale Song: A Celebration of Counting.* Putnam, 1987. **1956** In this simple story with beautiful illustrations, whales count as they sing. The mathematics focus is the use of number words.	F	K–3	I
Jonas, Ann. *Round Trip.* Morrow, 1990. **1957** Both reflections and tessellations enhance descriptions of a trip; a return trip is possible when this book is turned upside down.	F	3–6	I
Juster, Norton. *The Dot and the Line: A Romance in Lower Mathematics.* Random House, 1977. **1958** This is a delightful, mathematical love story. The straight line is in love with a frivolous dot, which in turn is attracted to an unkempt squiggle. The line finally learns how to bend and create many geometric shapes to attract the dot. Naturally, this story has a happy ending.	F	6–12	I
Juster, Norton. *The Phantom Tollbooth.* Knopf, 1988. **1959** Words are sold as a commodity in this fantasy world that includes many events related to mathematics.	SF	3–9	I
Kaplan, Andrew. *Careers for Number Lovers.* Millbrook, 1991. **1960** The personal accounts of people whose work involves mathematics introduces career possibilities to students who love numbers.	NFI	3–6	P
Kellogg, Steven. *Much Bigger Than Martin.* Dial, 1978. **1961** Order, measurement, and problem solving are addressed in a situation that is familiar to all younger siblings.	F	K–3	I
Kent, Jack. *Twelve Days of Christmas.* Parents' Magazine, 1973. **1962** As Christmas gifts accumulate, the focus is on counting them and predicting the total number of presents that will be received during the 12 days of Christmas.	F	K–3	I

	Type of literature	Grade span	Illus-trations

Kitchen, Bert. *Animal Numbers.* Dial, 1987.

| | F | K–3 | I |

1963 Each illustration has an Arabic number, an animal mother, and her babies. The enchanting drawings encourage young readers to count all of the different babies.

Klein, Leonore. *What Is an Inch?* Harvey House, 1966.

| | NFI | K–6 | I |

1964 In this book interesting, real-life situations lead students through the history and wonders of measurement with a delightful and logical mix of standard and nonstandard measurement.

Laithwaite, Eric. *Size: The Measure of Things.* Franklin Watts, 1988.

| | NFI | 3–6 | I |

1965 Written in a narrative style, this book excels in suggesting mental pictures of large sizes. The illustrations further clarify concepts such as scaling, relative size, growth, and complexity.

Le Sieg, Theo. *Ten Apples up on Top.* Beginner, 1961.

| | F | K–3 | I |

1966 The mathematical focus is on counting, addition, subtraction, number comparisons, and equations as three animals try to outdo each other in balancing apples on their heads.

Lieber, Lillian. *The Education of T. C. Mits.* Norton, 1944.

| | NFN | 6–12 | I |

1967 This book illuminates basic mathematical understandings. Each chapter begins with a practical example and ends with a moral. It is written in free verse and illustrated with imaginative line drawings.

Limmer, Milly J. *Where Will You Swim Tonight?* Edited by Ann Fay. Whitman, 1990.

| | F | K–3 | I |

1968 In this fantasy counting book, a young girl is turned into a fish. Every night she swims with one knobby sea horse, two smooth dolphins, and so forth, up to ten floppy penguins.

Linn, Charles F. *The Golden Mean: Mathematics and the Fine Arts.* Doubleday, 1974.

| | NFI | 9–12 | I |

1969 The author develops the theme that both mathematics and fine arts reflect the order in nature. His theory is based on examples from the time of the ancient Greeks to the present. This book is lavishly illustrated.

Lionni, Leo. *Pezzettino.* Pantheon, 1975.

| | F | K–6 | I |

1970 This book explores fractions, patterns, and relative sizes through the character of Pezzettino ("little piece," in Italian), who feels that he must be a part of something larger. Then he discovers that he is made up of even smaller pieces.

Lottridge, Celia. *One Watermelon Seed.* Oxford, 1990.

| | F | K–3 | I |

1971 A little boy and girl count the seeds they plant in a spring garden.

Lowery, Lawrence F. *How Tall Was Milton?* Holt, Rinehart and Winston, 1969.

| | F | K–3 | I |

1972 The mathematical focus is on estimates, standard measures, and accurate measurements. This good-humored story has the villagers trying to find a way to determine the height of their giant, Milton.

Macaulay, David. *Pyramid.* Houghton Mifflin, 1982.

| | NFI | 3–6 | I |

1973 The complex mathematical processes involved in building an Egyptian pyramid are described, including those for taking measurements and making geometrical calculations.

	Type of literature	Grade span	Illustrations
McMillan, Bruce. *Counting Wildflowers.* Lothrop, Lee and Shepard, 1986.	NFI	K–3	P
1974 An excellent integration of mathematics, science, and art, this counting book has photographs of 20 colorful wildflowers native to North America.			
McMillan, Bruce. *Time to . . .* Lothrop, Lee and Shepard, 1989.	NFI	K–3	P
1975 This introduction to telling time follows a farm boy through his day. Large clock faces and digital displays on the left-hand pages correspond to the times and activities described in the text.			
Maestro, Betsy. *Harriet Goes to the Circus.* Crown Publishers, 1989.	F	K–3	I
1976 Ordinal numbers are the mathematical focus as Harriet and the other animals line up for the circus.			
Maestro, Betsy. *Around the Clock with Harriet.* Crown Publishers, 1984.	NFI	K–3	I
1977 Harriet is followed through a 12-hour day. Both traditional clock faces and digital displays are used to teach children to tell time.			
Mahy, Margaret. *When the King Rides By.* Multimedia International, 1986.	F	K–3	I
1978 The rhythmic repetition of the text and the growing numbers of colorful people and animals in the King's procession encourage counting.			
Mathews, Louise. *Bunches and Bunches of Bunnies.* Dodd, Mead, 1978.	NFI	3–6	I
1979 Both multiplication and beginning word problems are introduced. In addition to bunnies, this book has bunches of rhymes and opportunities for adding and multiplying.			
Mathews, Louise. *Gator Pie.* Dodd, Mead, 1979.	F	K–6	I
1980 The mathematical focus is on fractions as the alligators divide a pie into smaller and smaller fractional parts.			
Mathews, Louise. *The Great Take-Away.* Dodd, Mead, 1980.	F	3–6	I
1981 A robber pig steals from fellow pigs, illustrating the concept of subtraction.			
Mathis, Sharon Bell. *Hundred Penny Box.* Viking, 1975.	F	3–9	I
1982 Michael loves the stories his great-aunt Dew tells as she pulls dated pennies from her box, one for each year of her life.			
Merrill, Jean. *The Toothpaste Millionaire.* Houghton Mifflin, 1974.	F	3–9	I
1983 In this warm, funny story, two friends who are good in mathematics discover that homemade toothpaste costs two cents a tube to produce. The mathematics class helps solve some of the real-life problems that are involved in starting a business and making a profit.			
Mori, Tuyosi. *Socrates and the Three Little Pigs.* Philomel, 1986.	F	3–9	I
1984 The mathematical focus is probability as the wolf, Socrates, tries to determine which house will yield the greatest number of tasty pigs.			
Myller, Rolf. *How Big Is a Foot?* Dell, 1990.	F	K–6	I
1985 This is an excellent look at both nonstandard and standard measurements. The importance of standard measurement is shown through the story of an apprentice who discovers that not all feet are the same size when a bed he builds for the Queen turns out to be too small for her.			

	Type of literature	Grade span	Illus- trations
Nozaki, Akihiro. *Anno's Hat Tricks.* Philomel, 1985. **1986** In this collection of simple and complex mathematical puzzles, the hypothetical *if* is given and the reader must deduce the *then.* This is a good book for sharing.	NFN	3–9	I
Ockenga, Starr, and Eileen Doolittle. *World of Wonders: A Trip Through Numbers.* Houghton Mifflin, 1988. **1987** This book for the observant child who likes details is filled with large illustrations with many things to count.	NFN	3–6	I
O'Neill, Mary. *Take a Number.* Doubleday, 1968. **1988** This long poem in free verse introduces readers to the vocabulary of numeration, geometry, sets, numbers, size comparisons, additive and commutative properties, and place values.	P	3–9	I
Owen, Annie. *Annie's One to Ten.* Knopf, 1989. **1989** This is more than a traditional counting book; the author demonstrates different ways to add up to ten.	F	K–3	I
Pappas, Theoni. *Math Talk: Mathematical Ideas in Poems for Two Voices.* World Tetra, 1991. **1990** This poetry examines many mathematical concepts in a fresh, interesting way.	P	9–12	I
Patent, Dorothy Hinshaw. *The Quest for Artificial Intelligence.* Harcourt Brace Jovanovich, 1986. **1991** The author presents the technological and philosophical issues surrounding artificial intelligence.	NFI	9–12	P
Paulos, John Allen. *Innumeracy: Mathematic Illiteracy and Its Consequences.* Hill and Wang, 1989. **1992** *Innumeracy* is the term for the inability to comprehend numbers and the inability to deal rationally with very large numbers. The author explores innumeracy and probes its impact on decision making at both personal and national levels.	NFI	9–12	
Paulos, John Allen. *Mathematics and Humor.* University of Chicago, 1982. **1993** The author takes the premise of a joke and breaks it down into a mathematical concept in this book.	NFN	9–12	
Pedoe, Dan. *Geometry and the Visual Arts.* Dover, 1983. **1994** The author discusses the enormous importance of geometry to Dürer, da Vinci, and Hobbs.	NFI	9–12	I
Peterson, Ivars. *The Mathematical Tourist: Snapshots of Modern Mathematics.* Freeman, 1989. **1995** Many interesting connections between mathematical abstractions and applications are given in this tour of Mathland. This book includes prime numbers, higher dimensions, factorials, map colors, topology, chaos, the game of life, and zero-knowledge proofs.	NFI	9–12	

	Type of literature	Grade span	Illus-trations
Phifer, Kate. **Tall and Small: A Book About Height.** Walker and Company, 1987. **1996** The author discusses growth patterns and explains how to chart growth. This book also addresses how people feel about their height.	NFI	3–9	I
Pinkwater, Daniel. **The Wuggie Norple Story.** Macmillan, 1988. **1997** This is a delightful read-aloud book with a funny and tongue-twisting text that explores perceptions, relative sizes, and comparisons.	F	K–6	I
Pittman, Helena Clare. **A Grain of Rice.** Hastings House, 1986. **1998** In this amusing story, a grain of rice is doubled each day, set in ancient China, resulting in a lot of rice in a short time.	F	3–9	I
Reid, Margarette. **The Button Box.** Dutton, 1990. **1999** As a boy plays with the buttons from the Button Box, he comments on their variety. The illustrations are organized so that it is easy to count buttons.	F	K–3	I
Reiss, John, Jr. **Shapes.** Macmillan, 1987. **2000** This book is a colorful introduction to squares, triangles, circles, rectangles, and ovals.	F	K–3	I
Riedel, Manfred G. **Winning with Numbers: A Kid's Guide to Statistics.** Prentice Hall, 1978. **2001** The author introduces delightful situations that demonstrate the power and pitfalls of the compilation of statistics, the presentation of facts, the language of statistics, and statistical by-products.	NFI	3–9	I
Ritchie, David. **The Computer Pioneers: The Making of the Modern Computer.** Simon and Schuster, 1986. **2002** The author presents the historical backgrounds of the mathematicians and engineers who are behind today's computer explosion. [Technology]	B	9–12	
Robart, Rose. **The Cake That Mack Ate.** Little, Brown, 1987. **2003** This humorous story follows all of the processes required to bake the beautiful birthday cake that Mack ate.	F	K–3	I
Rucker, Rudy. **Mind Tools: The Five Levels of Mathematical Reality.** Houghton Mifflin, 1988. **2004** The author groups the patterns of mathematics into five areas: number, space, logic, infinity, and information. This wide-ranging discussion of current mathematics is highly abstract but exciting for the able and interested student.	NFI	9–12	I
Sachar, Louis. **Sideways Arithmetic from Wayside School.** Scholastic, 1989. **2005** In this continuation of stories from Wayside School, everyone tries to solve puzzles that are based on both logic and mathematics. The answers and explanations are included at the end of the book.	F	6–9	
Schwartz, David M. **How Much Is a Million?** Scholastic, 1986. **2006** The concept of large numbers is introduced and pondered using illustrations of items familiar to a child. In the last pages, the author clearly explains how the calculations are done.	NFI	K–6	I

	Type of literature	Grade span	Illustrations
Schwartz, David M. *If You Made a Million.* Lothrop, Lee and Shepard, 1989. **2007** Photographs of real coins and bills are used to explain money and the uses of money. The author also cleverly explains borrowing, interest, checks, and services that banks provide.	NFN	3–9	I
Sendak, Maurice. *One Was Johnny.* Harper, 1962. **2008** This is a miniature counting book that goes up to ten and back down again. There are many rhymes in this whimsical story.	F	K–3	I
Shannon, George. *Stories to Solve: Folktales from Around the World.* Greenwillow, 1985. **2009** These 14 folktales include mysterious problems to solve. The notes have information about the countries, the sources, and the solutions.	NFN	6–12	I
Sharmat, Marjorie Weinman. *The 329th Friend.* Four Winds, 1979. **2010** The mathematics focus is counting by twos, threes, fours, and fives as a raccoon invites his friends to lunch.	F	K–3	I
Sitomer, Mindel, and Harry Sitomer. *How Did Numbers Begin?* Harper, 1976. **2011** In showing the origin and development of numbers, this book covers the concepts of *as many as, more than, less than, naming, ordering,* and *counting.*	NFI	K–6	I
Smith, George. *Mathematics: The Language of Science.* Putnam, 1961. **2012** This text is scientific and, at the same time, understandable. The author integrates the answers and then helps us see mathematics as a language.	NFN	3–9	I
Spohn, Kate. *Clementine's Winter Wardrobe.* Orchard Books, 1989. **2013** Clementine assembles and counts all the clothing she needs for winter.	F	K–6	I
Srivastava, Jane. *Number Families.* Crowell, 1979. **2014** By building on youngsters' understanding of families, the author introduces the concepts of *evens, odds, multiples, squares,* and *primes.*	NFI	3–6	I
Srivastava, Jane. *Spaces, Shapes, and Sizes.* Harper, 1980. **2015** The author explores the concept of volume and its relation to size and shape by depicting amusing animals in funny situations.	NFN	3–6	I
Srivastava, Jane. *Statistics.* Harper, 1973. **2016** In this introduction to statistics, the author explains the gathering of information, different types of graphs, and the uses of statistics.	NFI	3–6	I
Stwertka, Eve, and Albert Stwertka. *Make It Graphic: Drawing Graphs for Science and Social Studies Projects.* Julian Messner, 1985. **2017** This excellent introduction to graphs covers both the preparation and reading of line graphs, bar graphs, pie charts, and pictographs.	NFI	6–12	I
Swift, Jonathan. *Gulliver's Travels.* Viking, 1990. **2018** This classic tale incorporates the mathematical concepts of measurement, spatial sense, and scaling.	F	9–12	I
Tafuri, Nancy. *Who's Counting?* Greenwillow, 1986. **2019** This counting book presents a variety of animals that are familiar to young children.	F	K–3	I

	Type of literature	Grade span	Illustrations
Tompert, Ann. *Grandfather Tang's Story.* Crown Publishers, 1990. **2020** In this story-within-a-story, Grandfather Tang uses tangrams to tell Little Soo a tale. A tangram pattern is included with a brief explanation of these ancient Chinese puzzles.	F	3–9	I
Van Allsburg, Chris. *Two Bad Ants.* Houghton Mifflin, 1988. **2021** Both the illustrations and the narration provide contrasts of scale as we follow the adventures of two ants in a kitchen.	F	K–6	I
Viorst, Judith. *Alexander, Who Used to Be Rich Last Sunday.* Macmillan, 1987. **2022** In this riches-to-rags story, Alexander faces the realities of money. He experiences the joy of spending, the decision making, and the frustration of never having quite enough. This book stimulates discussions about the denominations of money and how it is used and managed.	F	K–3	I
Wahl, John, and Stacey Wahl. *I Can Count the Petals of a Flower.* National Classroom Teachers of Mathematics, 1985. **2023** The beautiful pictures of flowers that introduce counting also encourage understanding of the more advanced concepts such as *evens, odds, primes, composites,* and *factors.*	NF	K–3	I
Ward, Cindy. *Cookie's Week.* Putnam, 1988. **2024** The days of the week are sequenced through Cookie's antics.	F	K–3	I
Watson, Clyde. *Binary Numbers.* Harper, 1977. **2025** The author very clearly explains the doubling numbers in the binary sequence, demonstrates how quickly they grow, and shows how to write the numerals. Using this information, he then produces an elementary introduction to computers.	NFI	3–6	I
Wildsmith, Brian. *The Twelve Days of Christmas.* Franklin Watts, 1972. **2026** The familiar Christmas song, brilliantly illustrated, provides dozens of applications to mathematics, such as counting, time frames, money, and problem solving.	F	K–6	I
Williams, Jay. *A Box Full of Infinity.* Grosset and Dunlap, 1970. **2027** The poor wizard will never bother anyone again because he is stuck trying to count beyond infinity. This classic tale of a damsel in distress features a very clever prince who uses mathematics to trick the wizard.	F	3–6	I
Young, Jeffrey S. *Steve Jobs: The Journey Is the Reward.* Lynx, 1988. **2028** This is the story of Steve Jobs—his successes, failures, and hopes for the future—and of his Apple Computer Company, which he began in a garage and developed into the fastest growing company in the history of Wall Street. [Technology]	B	9–12	
Zaslavsky, Claudia. *Africa Counts.* Hill, 1979. **2029** This is a fascinating look at the uses of numbers and counting throughout Africa.	NFI	6–12	I
Zolotow, Charlotte. *One Step, Two . . .* Lothrop, Lee and Shepard, 1981. **2030** The mathematical focus is on the importance of the process as a little girl takes her mother on a "counting walk," sharing the joys of discovering and observing ordinary things.	F	K–6	I

Selected Methods for Using Literature in the Science Class

This publication is grounded in the belief that the inherent richness of the science classroom can be greatly enhanced through the use of literature. Literature can not only inform students of the facts of a specific subject or topic but it can also extend students' limited personal experience. Because literature creates images for readers, it can transport them to a different time and place. Such vicarious experiences can help students to understand the connections between science and culture, to participate in the major discoveries of science, and to correlate an object with its name. Through literature, students can participate in scientific activities as varied as the design of superconducting monorails and the production of artificial chocolate with no calories.

Although the main purpose of this publication is to provide educators, parents, and librarians with lists of literature that is recommended for the science classroom, it also includes suggestions as to how this literature might be used:

◆ In the early grades, students lack the background necessary to fully comprehend scientific concepts or to visualize objects or creatures they have never seen. For example, it is very difficult for a young student to invoke a mental picture of a bison when he or she has never seen one. By studying the pictures and photographs in books, however, students can make connections between the object, its image, and its name. Then *bison* becomes not just a meaningless word to memorize but a large, oxlike animal. Literature can also tell a story that provides the background knowledge that is so essential for understanding abstract principles.

◆ Students who are reading literature to enhance their knowledge in a certain area of their science class should be given the opportunity to share their information with classmates. Such sharing might be done in discussion groups or through individual reports to the class.

◆ Through the use of literature, students can be asked to apply critical thinking skills to complex subjects such as nuclear power. The students will learn much about both the advantages and the disadvantages of using nuclear power.

◆ High-quality science-related literature can motivate students to study subjects that are intrinsically interesting to them. The colorful and lively formats of many of these books make expanding their scientific knowledge enjoyable. Two examples follow:

- In the primary classroom, children enjoy learning about animals and their habits. *Animals Born Alive and Well,* by Ruth Heller, introduces the characteristics of mammals for further study.

- Sixth grade students can write a response to the question: "If the dinosaur did, in fact, evolve into a present-day animal, which one would it be and why?" Then the elementary book *The News About Dinosaurs,* by Patricia Lauber, can be read to them, challenging them to rethink what they wrote about the relationships between present-day and prehistoric animals.

◆ In addition to reading, writing should also be an integral part of the science program. Through innovative research reports, presentations, and experiments, students can be asked to share the knowledge they have acquired through reading. Also, working cooperatively or independently, students become problem solvers, critical thinkers, and decision makers.

- *Machines at Work,* by Byron Barton, will inspire primary students to create their own machines and write descriptions about how they function. Joanne Ryder's simple and elegant story *The Snail's Spell,* written from a snail's perspective, can provide elementary students with a different model for a research report on animals. Students might then write their own stories from an animal's perspective.

- Older students will enjoy writing books for younger students on rock collecting after reading *Rock Collecting,* by Roma Gans, and *Everybody Needs a Rock,* by Byrd Baylor.

◆ Teachers can develop a science lesson that provides both scientific information and reinforcement by using a science-related literature book.

- For primary and elementary classrooms, *The Sun, the Wind, and the Rain,* by Lisa Westberg Peters, can be used to reinforce lessons on the formation of mountains and erosion from the elements. Students in the intermediate and high school grades can learn and investigate how ocean currents affect seashores by reading *The Big Wave,* by Pearl Buck, for intermediate students, or Rachel Carson's *The Sea Around Us*, for high school students. Each of these books deals with *tsunamis,* or tidal waves.

◆ After reading the following books, students can be asked to compare and contrast ideas, make conjectures, and suggest hypotheses in classroom discussions:

- *Dinosaurs Walked Here: And Other Stories Fossils Tell,* by Patricia Lauber (3–6)

- *Digging Dinosaurs,* by John Horner and James Gorman (9–12)

- *Earth Story,* by Eric Maddern (K–3)

- *A Shovelful of Earth,* by Lorus and Margery Milne (6–12)

- *Universe: Past, Present and Future,* by David Darling (6–9)

◆ One of the major outcomes of science education should be that students understand more fully the features of their everyday lives. To this end, books about things, people, and places that are familiar or relevant to students can be used, such as the following:

- Things:

  A Tree Is Nice, by Janice Udry (K–3)

  Apple Tree, by Peter Parnall (3–6)

  The Big Tree, by Bruce Hiscock (3–6)

- People:

  What Are Scientists? What Do They Do? by Rita Golden Gelman (K–3)

The Glorious Flight Across the Channel with Louis Bleriot, by Alice and Martin Provensen (3–6)

The Wright Brothers: How They Invented the Airplane, by Russell Freedman (6–9)

The Cuckoo's Egg: Inside the World of Computer Espionage, by Clifford Stoll (9–12)

- Places:

A Forest Is Reborn, by James Newton (3–6)

The Secret House, by David Bodanis (9–12)

◆ The following books emphasize observation and can be used to promote activities inside and outside the classroom:

- *The Oak Tree,* by Laura Jane Coats (K–3)

- *Guess Who My Favorite Person Is?* by Byrd Baylor (3–9)

- *Where Butterflies Grow,* by Joanne Ryder (K–6)

- *Crinkleroot's Book of Animal Tracking,* by Jim Arnosky (3–9)

◆ Reading aloud can be a good teaching technique at any grade level and with any size group. Some uses of this technique are:

- To introduce a new topic or lesson

- To reinforce previously covered material

- To expand scientific concepts

- To settle down a class before beginning a lesson

A Lesson Plan Using Literature

The following two-day lesson plan for a primary class shows more specifically how literature might be integrated into science lessons. This lesson might cover several hours each day and might be the beginning of the study of weather over a longer period of time. The plan contains components of curricula other than science to demonstrate further how other content areas might be integrated with science. The plan incorporates use of the book *Weather Words and What They Mean,* by Gail Gibbons, which clearly defines the factors that influence weather and the terms used to describe different types of weather. The goals of the lesson would be to have students demonstrate and build on prior knowledge of weather terms and to begin related weather activities.

Day One

Needed: Chart paper, several newspapers from different publishers, various types of thermometers (e.g., room, outdoor, oven, meat, laboratory, and medical thermometers)

1. In order to understand students' current perceptions, the teacher asks them what they think *weather* means. Depending on their ages and abilities, either they write their own responses or the teacher writes them on chart paper.

2. As a brainstorming activity, the teacher asks the students for words related to weather and writes them on chart paper. The teacher and children then group words according to the type of weather they describe. Various groups of words can be written on separate pieces of chart paper. Students then draw pictures suggested by the words and display them around the classroom.

3. The teacher reads the book to the children, possibly in two parts to allow time for discussion. The children and teacher add new words to the charts using a different color pen.

4. The teacher shows the weather reports in each of the newspapers, reads parts of the reports, and identifies familiar words. The teacher identifies differences and similarities among the reports and points out interesting weather in other parts of the world.

5. The teacher introduces the various thermometers. The class discusses the uses of each thermometer. Which is for studying weather? Where would you measure air temperature to study weather (indoors, outdoors, in the shade, in an air-conditioned room, in the sun)?

6. The class discusses the best places and times for measuring the air temperature to study changes in the weather. The teacher prepares charts to record temperatures and weather observations.

Day Two

Needed: Indoor thermometers, outdoor thermometers, supplies for students' journals, magazines and newspapers with weather pictures

1. The teacher gives students materials for a weather log, in which they will record temperatures and weather observations. Students can illustrate the covers of their logs or individualize them in other ways.

2. The class performs the temperature measurements as discussed on the first day. Ideally, groups of children would measure the temperature at various times of the day in one of a variety of places, such as in shady or sunny places, over pavement, and over grass. The times, places, and temperatures are recorded on the class chart and in each child's log.

3. Students cut out pictures from magazines and newspapers for two weather collages. They choose pictures that show harmful or helpful effects of weather. Students glue pictures illustrating helpful effects onto one large sheet of paper and those illustrating harmful effects onto another. Then, students use either collage as the basis of a written response to one of the following questions: How is weather helpful? How is it harmful?

4. For homework, students watch the weather report on the television news.

This publication lists many books related to weather topics. They can be found through the subject index.

Thematic Teaching

According to the *Science Framework for California Public Schools,* "the themes of science are ideas that integrate the concepts of different scientific disciplines in ways that are useful to the presentation and teaching of scientific content." The *Science Framework* develops six such themes: energy, evolution, patterns of change, scales and structure, stability, and systems and interactions.

The basic building blocks of science, however, are not themes but theories. As defined in the *Science Framework*, a theory is "an explanation or model based on observation, experimentation, and reasoning, especially one that has been tested and confirmed as a general principle helping to explain and predict natural phenomena." Theories connect concepts within a scientific discipline: themes can connect ideas across disciplines.

The *Science Framework* encourages educators to weave themes into science curricula. However, the sequence of concepts should be based on such factors as the students' interests, their readiness to learn, their previous knowledge, and the theory-based structure of science. Although this publication does not identify the themes in the titles it recommends, science teachers will recognize themes in the literature they select. If, after presenting a particular book, a teacher asks, for example, "What ideas about energy are included?" examples can likely be found. Similar questions could be posed for several of the themes developed in the *Science Framework*. In any particular book, the relationship between some themes might be more apparent than for others, however. The following example illustrates how thematic teaching might progress.

Gail Gibbons's *Seeds* traces the life cycle of a plant, with a special emphasis on the role of seeds and a plant's methods of producing them. Since the focus of the book is on the cycle of growth from the germination of a seed to the production of a new seed, the main theme might be thought of as "patterns of change." But the "scale and structure" of plants is almost as important in this book, and "systems and interactions" with insects and other animals is also clearly evident. The theme of "energy" also comes into play in a plant's production of and use of food. The book does not, however, deal overtly with "evolution" or "stability."

Another book by Gibbons, *Sun Up, Sun Down*, is about the sun, clouds, rain, and rainbows. In addition to pointing out the theoretical connection between plant growth and the sun, the teacher using this book after *Seeds* can relate the "patterns of change" in the sun's daily and yearly cycles to the life cycles of plants in the previous book. By using this theme, then, the teacher has shown the scientific similarity between the life cycle of plants and the planetary movement of the earth.

Thematic teaching requires that teachers know science well enough to understand the relationships between concepts. This knowledge can be acquired gradually, and its application to the classroom can greatly enhance the teaching of science.

Selected Resource Materials

The main purpose of this document is to recommend science-related literature to educators. However, there are many useful resources that are not literature but are important scientific publications. This appendix is organized to give as much information about these publications as possible. The entries are divided into four categories: Reference Books; Field Guides; Books on Activities, Projects, and Experiments; and Miscellaneous Publications. Annotations are supplied when needed, as well as the recommended grade spans.

Reference Books

These books include dictionaries of science, alphabetized compilations of interesting scientific facts, and lists of scientists that include biographical data.

	Grade span
The Biographical Dictionary of Scientists: Astronomers. Edited by David Abbott. Bedrick, 1984.	6–12
The Biographical Dictionary of Scientists: Biologists. Edited by David Abbott. Bedrick, 1984.	6–12
The Biographical Dictionary of Scientists: Chemists. Edited by David Abbott. Bedrick, 1984.	6–12
The Biographical Dictionary of Scientists: Physicists. Edited by David Abbott. Bedrick, 1984.	6–12
Book of Science and Nature Quotations. Edited by Isaac Asimov and Jason A. Shulman. Grove Weidenfeld, 1989.	9–12
Cazeau, Charles J. *Science Trivia: From Anteaters to Zeppelins.* Plenum, 1986.	9–12
Cox, James A. *The Endangered Ones.* Crown Publishers, 1975.	9–12

Cox, P. A. *The Elements: Their Origin, Abundance and Distribution.* Oxford, 1989. 9–12

Flatlow, Ira. *Rainbows, Curve Balls: And Other Wonders of the Natural World Explored.* Harper, 1988. 6–12

Golob, Richard. *Almanac of Science and Technology: What's New and What's Known.* Harbrace, 1990. 9–12

Field Guides

Some of the best guides to the natural and physical world are included in this category to help teachers select materials for their students that other young people have found most interesting, accurate, and accessible.

Grade span

Alt, David D., and Donald Hyndman. *Roadside Geology of Northern California.* Mountain Press, 1975. 9–12

Audubon Society Staff. *Audubon Society Field Guide: North American Wildflowers, Western Region.* Knopf, 1979. 3–9

Audubon Society Staff, and Charles W. Chesterman. *Audubon Society Field Guide to North American Rocks and Minerals.* Knopf, 1979. 3–9

Audubon Society Staff, and Elbert L. Little, Jr. *Audubon Field Guide to North American Trees (Western Region).* Knopf, 1980. 3–9

Audubon Society Staff, and F. Wayne King. *Audubon Society Field Guide to North American Reptiles and Amphibians.* Knopf, 1979. 3–9

Audubon Society Staff, and Gary H. Lincoff. *Audubon Society Field Guide to North American Mushrooms.* Knopf, 1981. 3–9

Audubon Society Staff, and Harold A. Rehder. *Audubon Society Field Guide to North American Seashells.* Knopf, 1981. 3–9

Audubon Society Staff, and Ida Thompson. *Audubon Society Field Guide to North American Fossils.* Knopf, 1982. 3–9

Audubon Society Staff, and John O. Whitaker. *Audubon Field Guide to North American Mammals.* Knopf, 1980. 3–9

Audubon Society Staff, and Lorus Milne. *Audubon Society Field Guide to North American Insects and Spiders.* Knopf, 1980. 3–9

Audubon Society Staff, and Norman A. Meinkoth. *Audubon Society Field Guide to North American Seashore Creatures.* Knopf, 1981. 3–9

Audubon Society Staff, and others. *Audubon Society Field Guide to North American Fishes, Whales, and Dolphins.* Knopf, 1983. 3–9

Audubon Society Staff, and Robert M. Pyle. *Audubon Society Field Guide to North American Butterflies.* Knopf, 1981. 3–9

Benyus, Janine M. *The Field Guide to Wildlife Habitats of the Western United States.* Simon and Schuster, 1989. 6–12

Brown, Lauren. *Grasslands.* Audubon Society Nature Guides series. Knopf, 1985. 6–12

Color Atlas of Human Anatomy. Edited by Vanio Vannini and Giuliano Pogliani. Crown Publishers, 1981. 9–12

Ehrlich, Paul R., David S. Dubkin, and Darryl Wheye. *The Birder's Handbook: A Field Guide to the Natural History of North American Birds.* Simon and Schuster, 1988. 6–12

Encyclopedia of Science and Technology. Twenty volumes, sixth edition. McGraw-Hill, 1987. 9–12

Gallant, Roy A. *The Macmillan Book of Astronomy.* Macmillan, 1986. 6–12

Garber, Steven D. *Urban Naturalist.* John Wiley, 1987. 6–12

Gardner, Robert. *The Whale Watchers' Guide.* Julian Messner, 1984. 6–12

Hatchett, Clint. *The Glow-in-the-Dark Night Sky Book.* Random House, 1988. 3–6

Herberman, Ethan. *The City Kid's Field Guide.* Simon and Schuster, 1989. 3–6

Jobb, Jamie. *Night Sky Book: An Everyday Guide to Every Night.* Little, Brown, 1977. 3–9

Johnson, Lady Bird, and Carlton B. Lees. *Wildflowers Across America.* Abbeville, 1988. 9–12

Keator, Glenn. *Pacific Coast Berry Finder.* Nature Study, 1978. 3–9

Keator, Glenn. *Sierra Flower Finder: A Guide to Sierra Nevada Wildflowers.* Nature Study, 1980. 3–9

Keator, Glenn, and Ruth Heady. *Pacific Coast Fern Finder.* Nature Study, 1978. 3–9

Lawrence, Gale. *Field Guide to the Familiar: Learning to Observe the Natural World.* Prentice-Hall, 1984. 3–9

Lederer, Roger. *Pacific Coast Bird Finder: A Manual for Identifying 61 Common Birds of the Pacific Coast.* Nature Study, 1973. 3–9

Lerner, Carol. *Dumb Cane and Daffodils: Poisonous Plants in the House and Garden.* William Morrow, 1990. 6–9

Lerner, Carol. *Moonseed and Mistletoe: A Book of Poisonous Wild Plants.* William Morrow, 1988. 6–9

Lerner, Carol. *Plant Families.* William Morrow, 1989. 3–9

Lilley, Bill, and Ben Meyer. *The Cambridge Atlas of Astronomy.* Second edition. Edited by Jean Audouze and Guy Israel. Cambridge, 1988. 9–12

MacMahon, James A. *Deserts.* Audubon Society Nature Guides series. Knopf, 1985. 6–12

Mitchell, Andrew. *Young Naturalist.* EDC, 1984. 9-12

National Audubon Society Staff. *Audubon's Birds of America.* Abbeville, 1989. 9–12

Niehaus, Theodore F. *Sierra Wildflowers: Mount Lassen to Kern Canyon.* 6–12
University of California, 1974.

Pough, Frederick H. *Peterson First Guide to Rocks and Minerals.* PETERSON 3–9
FIRST GUIDE series. Houghton Mifflin, 1991.

Pyke, Magnus. *Weird and Wonderful Science Facts.* Sterling, 1985. 6–9

Rawson, Christopher, and Colin King. *How Machines Work.* Usborne House, 1988. 6–9

Robbins, Chandler S.; Bertel Bruun; and Herbert S. Zim. *Birds of North* 3–9
America: A Guide to Field Identification. Western Publishing, 1981.

Room, Adrian. *The Guinness Book of Numbers.* Facts on File, 1991. K–12

Russo, Ron, and Pam Olhousen. *Pacific Intertidal Life.* Nature Study, 1981. 3–9

Spurgeon, Richard. *Energy and Power.* EDC, 1990. 6–12

Stein, Sara. *The Evolution Book.* Workman, 1986. 6–12

Stein, Sara. *The Science Book.* Workman, 1980. 9–12

Storer, Tracy I., and Robert L. Usinger. *Sierra Nevada Natural History: An* 6–12
Illustrated Handbook. University of California, 1963.

Supraner, Robyn. *Science Secrets.* Troll, 1981. K–6

Thompson, C. E. *Glow-in-the-Dark Constellations: A Field Guide for Young* 3–9
Stargazers. Putnam, 1989.

Vessel, Matthew F., and Herbert H. Wong. *Natural History of a Vacant Lot.* 6–12
University of California, 1988.

Watts, Tom. *Pacific Coast Tree Finder: A Manual for Identifying Pacific Coast* 3–9
Trees. Nature Study, 1973.

Whitney, Stephen. *Western Forests.* Edited by Charles Elliot. Knopf, 1985. 6–12

Books on Activities, Projects, and Experiments

These books were chosen to help students learn safe methods of experimentation, scientific thinking, and creativity. Some of these activity books were originally published in England, and unfamiliar word usage may present some difficulties to students. Therefore, teachers should be prepared to assist students.

Grade span

Abruscato, Joe, and Jack Hassard. *The Whole Cosmos Catalog of Science* 3–6
Activities for Kids of All Ages. Scott, Foresman, 1977.
This book includes a variety of fascinating hands-on activities and projects that
encompass many scientific fields and create a desire to learn more about our world.

Allison, Linda, and David Katz. *Gee, Wiz! How to Mix Art and Science:* 3–9
Or the Art of Thinking Scientifically. Yolla Bolly, 1983.
This book explains the underlying scientific principles for a variety of experiments,
projects, and activities.

Arnosky, Jim. *Drawing from Nature.* William Morrow, 1991.   6–9
>The author gives instructions for drawing and introduces techniques for sharpening observational skills and developing an appreciation of the order and structure of nature.

Arnosky, Jim. *Drawing Life in Motion.* William Morrow, 1991.   6–9
>The author provides detailed instructions for drawing the movements of wild creatures and for sketching a variety of leaves. At the same time, he emphasizes the scientific observational skills one needs when drawing from nature.

Arnosky, Jim. *Sketching Outdoors in Autumn.* Lothrop, Lee and Shepard, 1988.   3–12
>The author introduces his techniques for sketching the characteristics of fall, such as animal tracks and leaves. Also see other books in this series on sketching outdoors in spring, summer, and winter.

Burns, Marilyn. *The I Hate Mathematics! Book.* Little Brown, 1975.   3–9
>Good humor and down-to-earth applications lead reluctant math students from fear to confidence through activities that are amplifications of the concepts presented in this book.

Burns, Marilyn. *The One-Dollar Word Riddle Book.* Cuisenaire, 1990.   3–9
>The atypical riddles in this book can be answered only by doing some mathematics.

Cobb, Vicki. *Lots of Rot.* Harper, 1981.   3–6
>The author explains the process of decomposition and the important roles played by mold, bacteria, and mildew. This book ends with suggestions for growing these "rotters."

Cobb, Vicki. *More Science Experiments You Can Eat.* Harper, 1984.   3–6
>The principles of chemistry and physics are introduced with experiments that make use of common kitchen ingredients. If these experiments are correctly conducted, the results are edible.

Cobb, Vicki. *Science Experiments You Can Eat.* Harper, 1972.   3–9
>Scientific principles are logically developed in this book of simple experiments that treat the kitchen as a well-equipped laboratory.

Cobb, Vicki. *The Secret Life of Cosmetics: A Science Experiment Book.* Harper 1985.   3–9
>This introduction to cosmetics includes their history and experiments to test cosmetic products before using them.

Durrell, Gerald, and Lee Durrell. *The Amateur Naturalist.* Knopf, 1983.   6–12
>The authors describe methods and environments that aspiring naturalists could use for their studies. They also discuss the history of this profession and its rewards.

Gardner, Robert. *Science Around the House.* Julian Messner, 1989.   3–9
>This book suggests a number of hands-on experiments and projects that make use of household materials and encourage thinking and observation about evaporation, gravity, friction, and light.

Headstrom, Richard. *Adventures with a Microscope.* Dover, 1977.   3–9
>The author describes objects and raises questions that challenge students to use a microscope to explore and investigate a variety of common, easily obtained items.

Kressen, David P. *Teach Your Computer to Think in BASIC.* Jacobs, 1983.   3–9
>This manual shows an upper elementary student how to begin programming a computer in the BASIC language.

Penrose, Gordon. *Magic Mud: The Best of Dr. Zed's Brilliant Science Activities and Other Great Experiments.* Simon and Schuster, 1988.   6–12
Using photographs and cartoons, the author cleverly explains numerous physical phenomena. The hands-on activities are explained in simple language.

Simon, Seymour. *How to Be an Ocean Scientist in Your Own Home.* Harper, 1988.   3–9
This collection of experiments is intended to increase knowledge about oceans and sea life.

Simon, Seymour. *Pets in a Jar: Collecting and Caring for Small Animals.* Puffin, 1979.   3–9
This book has suggestions for collecting 15 small creatures that will survive in a gallon jar, observing them, and then releasing them.

Simon, Seymour. *Shadow Magic.* Lothrop, 1985.   K–6
This book leads students into a study of light, angles, objects, and their shadows. Students may apply their knowledge to shadow clocks and sundials, or they may explore the "lighter" side of shadows through finger plays.

Smith, Norman. *How to Do Successful Science Projects.* Revised edition by Jane Steltenpohl. (Previous title, *How Fast Do Your Oysters Grow?*) Julian Messner, 1990.   9–12
The author describes how scientists work as he explains the steps in a science project. He addresses planning the investigation, choosing the equipment and the test procedures, recording the data, drawing conclusions, and reporting the results.

Walpole, Brenda. *175 Science Experiments to Amuse and Amaze Your Friends.* Random House, 1988.   3–9
This book begins with tips on how to be a scientist and proceeds with activities and explanations.

White, Laurence. *Math-a-Magic: Number Tricks for Magicians.* Whitman, 1990.   3–6
This book introduces enjoyable number tricks for young children.

Wyler, Rose. *Science Fun with Peanuts and Popcorn.* Julian Messner, 1985.   K–6
Peanuts and popcorn are introduced in this book that includes their histories and hands-on activities that range from growing plants to preparing simple recipes.

Wyler, Rose. *Science Fun with Mud and Dirt.* Julian Messner, 1986.   K–6
This introduction to soil and dirt explains the different types and colors and discusses the creatures that live in the soil. A number of hands-on experiments use easily obtained materials.

Wyler, Rose. *Science Fun with Toy Boats and Planes.* Julian Messner, 1989.   K–6
The scientific principles of flotation, displacement, weight, gravity, action, reaction, and aerodynamics are introduced through homemade boats and planes. The hands-on experiments use easily obtained materials.

Zubrowski, Bernie. *A Children's Museum Activity Book: Bubbles.* Little, Brown, 1979.   3–9
Hands-on activities provide fun with bubbles.

Zubrowski, Bernie. *Messing Around with Baking Chemistry: A Children's Museum Activity Book.* Little, Brown, 1981.   3–9
This is a hands-on book of experiments that introduce the peculiar properties of baking soda, baking powder, and yeast.

Zubrowski, Bernie. *Messing Around with Water Pumps and Siphons: A Children's Museum Activity Book.* Little, Brown, 1981. 3–9
    Hands-on experiments illustrate the principles of suction and compression with the use of water pumps and siphons.

Zubrowski, Bernie. *Raceways: Having Fun with Balls and Tracks.* William Morrow, 1985. 3–9
    Hands-on activities introduce the scientific principles of gravity, momentum, and kinetic energy.

Zubrowski, Bernie. *Tops: Building and Experimenting with Spinning Toys.* William Morrow, 1989. 3–9
    Hands-on activities include the use of different shapes and materials for building toys such as tops and yo-yos.

Zubrowski, Bernie. *Wheels at Work.* William Morrow, 1986. 3–6
    Hands-on activities introduce pulleys, windlasses, and water wheels.

Miscellaneous Publications

This small group of books, which do not fit any specific category, may also be of interest to students.

Grade span

Aaseng, Nathan. *Better Mousetraps: Product Improvements That Led to Success.* Lerner, 1989. 3–9
    The eight creative people who are introduced in the book refined and improved products that make our lives easier and safer.

Bourgeois, Paulette. *The Amazing Paper Book.* Addison-Wesley, 1990. 3–9
    The history, uses, and effects on modern life of paper are all wonderfully integrated in this intriguing book. The activities are enjoyable, interesting, and irresistible.

Caduto, Michael, and Joseph Bruchac. *Keepers of the Earth: Native American Stories and Environmental Activities for Children.* Fulcrum, 1988. 3–12
    Oral history, legends, and myths emphasize the Native American belief in preserving the chain of life.

DeWaard, E. John, and Nancy DeWaard. *History of NASA: America's Voyage to the Stars.* Exeter, 1984. 6–12

Gratzer, Walter. *Literary Companion to Science.* Norton, 1990. 9–12
    This anthology is arranged by broad scientific topics that include poetry, short stories, and book excerpts.

Kent, Amanda, and Alan Ward. *Introduction to Physics.* Basic Guides series. EDC, 1984. 6–12
    This book defines physics, discusses the types of energy, and explains the forces that cause movement or pressure. The many examples are illustrated with drawings that enhance the text.

Lattimer, Dick. *All We Did Was Fly to the Moon.* Whispering Eagle Press, 1985. 6–12
    This book presents information on each space mission from the first *Mercury* mission through the *Apollo* and *Skylab* missions.

Pogue, William R. *How Do You Go to the Bathroom in Space?* Tor, 1985. 6–12

The author, who flew with two *Apollo* missions and *Skylab 4,* uses a question-and-answer format to address the serious and not-so-serious questions many people have always had about living and working in space.

Spurgeon, R. *Ecology.* EDC, 1989. 6–12

The basic concepts of ecology are introduced, including ecosystems, food chains, and adaptations. The hands-on projects are fascinating and enjoyable.

Index of Subjects

(The numbers below correspond to the numbers assigned to specific titles.)

Index of Authors

A

Aardema, Verna   22
Aaseng, Nathan   2
Abbott, Edwin   86
Abrams, Lawrence F.   2
Adams, Adrienne   2
Adamson, Joy   42
Adams, Pam   86
Adkins, Jan   2
Adler, David   86
Adler, David A.   42
Adler, Irving   86
Adshead, Paul   42
Aker, Suzanne   86
Albers, Donald J.   86
Alexanderson, G. L.   86
Aliki   22, 42
Allen, Joseph P.   22
Allen, Pamela   87
Allison, Linda   2, 22, 42
Alpers, Antony   42
Alvarez, Luis W.   2
Ancona, George   42
Anderson, Byron D.   17
Anderson, Lucia   43
Anno, Mitsumasa   22, 87
Apfel, Necia H.   2
Archambault, John   33
Ardley, Neil   3, 87
Argent, Kerry   88
Arnold, Caroline   22, 43, 44
Arnosky, Jim   44
Arthur, Alex   44
Asch, Frank   3
Ashabranner, Brent   88
Ashabranner, Melissa   88
Asimov, Isaac   3, 23, 44
Atkins, Peter W.   3
Attenborough, David   44
Aylesworth, Thomas G.   3
Ayres, Pam   44

B

Back, Christine   44, 45
Baines, John   23
Baker, Jeannie   45
Baker, Olaf   45
Bakker, Robert T.   23
Ballard, J. G.   23

Ballard, Robert D.   23
Balzola, Asun   23
Bang, Molly   88
Bannan, Jan Gumprecht   23
Bare, Colleen Stanley   45
Barton, Byron   3
Base, Graeme   88
Bash, Barbara   45
Baum, Arline   3
Baum, Joseph   3
Baylor, Byrd   23, 45
Bear, Greg   46
Beattie, Owen   23
Becker, John   88
Beckmann, Petr   88
Bee, Ronald J.   7
Beer, Stafford   4
Bellamy, David   46
Bendick, Jeanne   88
Benford, Gregory   3
Bennett, David   23, 24
Berger, Melvin   3, 24, 46
Berry, Louise   34
Beshore, George   4
Billings, Charlene   4
Bishop, Owen   88
Bjork, Christina   46
Blegvad, Lenore   88
Blocksma, Mary   88
Blohm, Hans   4
Bodanis, David   46
Bonners, Susan   46
Borden, Louise   24
Bourne, Geoffrey H.   46
Bova, Ben   24
Bowermaster, Jon   38
Boyne, Walter J.   4
Boynton, Sandra   89
Brady, Irene   46
Brand, Stewart   4
Branley, Franklyn M.   4, 24, 25, 46, 89
Brenner, Barbara   47
Brenner, Martha   5
Brett, Jan   47
Briggs, Raymond   89
Brin, David   25
Broekel, Ray   18
Bronowski, Jacob   5
Brooks, Bruce   47
Brothwell, Don   47
Brown, A. E.   5

Stewart, George   80
Stoll, Clifford   17
Stolz, Mary   80
Stone, A. Harris   17
Stone, Lynne   80
Strieber, Whitley   80
Strum, Shirley C.   80
Sturgeon, Theodore   80
Stwertka, Albert   99
Stwertka, Eve   99
Sussman, Susan   80
Suzuki, David   4
Swift, Jonathan   99
Symes, R. F.   38

T

Tafuri, Nancy   99
Taylor, Theodore   38
Tchudi, Stephen   17
Tepper, Sheri S.   80
Thomas, Lewis   81
Titherington, Jeanne   81
Todd, Frank   81
Tokuda, Wendy   81
Tompert, Ann   100
Torres, George   38
Toye, William   81
Trefil, James   18, 38
Trinca, Rod   88
Tucker, Karen   18
Tucker, Wallace   18
Turner, Ann   81
Tuttle, Merlin D.   81

U

Udry, Janice May   81

V

Van Allsburg, Chris   38, 100
Van Soelen, Philip   82
Vare, Ehtlie   38
Vassilissa   82
Vendrell, Carme Sole   38, 39
Verne, Jules   39
Vinge, Joan D.   82
Viorst, Judith   100
Vogel, Carole   82

W

Wahl, John   100
Wahl, Stacey   100
Wakefield, Pat   82

Walters, Mark Jerome   82
Ward, Cindy   100
Watson, Clyde   100
Watson, James D.   82
Watson, Lyall   18, 39
Watts, Barrie   45, 82, 83
Weaver, Harriett E.   83
Weinberg, Steven   18
Weiner, Jonathan   39
Weir, David   18
Weissmann, Gerald   83
Weitzman, David   18
Wertheim, Anne   83
Westberg-Peters, Lisa   83
White, Jack R.   18
White, Laurence B.   18
Whitfield, Philip   39
Wiesner, David   39
Wiewandt, Thomas   83
Wilcox, Charlotte   39
Wildsmith, Brian   83, 100
Wilkins, Malcolm   83
Will, Clifford M.   18
Williams, Gene B.   39
Williams, Jay   100
Williamson, Ray A.   34
Williams, Terry   39
Wilson, Dorothy Clarke   83
Winckler, Suzanne   40
Wold, Allen L.   90
Wolf, Fred Alan   19
Wolfe, Tom   18
Woods, Geraldine   19
Wren, M. K.   83
Wright, Helen   40
Wright, Joan R.   71
Wyndham, John   84

Y

Yeager, Chuck   19
Yolen, Jane   84
Yoshida, Toshi   84
Young, Carolyn   35
Young, Jeffrey S.   100
Yue, Charlotte   84
Yue, David   84

Z

Zaslavsky, Claudia   100
Zolotow, Charlotte   100

Index of Titles

M

Y

Z

Publications Available from the Department of Education

This publication is one of over 600 that are available from the California Department of Education. Some of the more recent publications or those related in subject matter are the following:

Item No.	Title (Date of publication)	Price
1063	Adoption Recommendations of the Curriculum Development and Supplemental Materials Commission, 1992: California Basic Instructional Materials in Science (1992)	$5.50
0972	California Assessment Program: A Sampler of Mathematics Assessment (1991)	5.00
0975	California Private School Directory, 1991-92 (1991)	16.00
1074	California Public School Directory (1993)	16.00
0488	Caught in the Middle: Educational Reform for Young Adolescents in California Public Schools (1987)	6.75
0777	The Changing Mathematics Curriculum: A Booklet for Parents (1989)	10/5.00*
0891	The Changing Mathematics Curriculum: A Booklet for Parents (Spanish Edition) (1991)	10/5.00*
0976	Economic Education Mandate: Handbook for Survival (1991)	7.75
0786	Enrichment Opportunities Guide: A Resource for Teachers and Students in Math and Science (with binder) (1988)	8.75†
9974	Everybody Counts: A Report to the Nation on the Future of Mathematics Education (1989)	5.00‡
0804	Foreign Language Framework for California Public Schools (1989)	6.50
0734	Here They Come: Ready or Not—Report of the School Readiness Task Force (Full Report) (1988)	5.50
0712	History–Social Science Framework for California Public Schools (1988)	7.75
1024	It's Elementary! Elementary Grades Task Force Report (1992)	6.50
1033	Mathematics Framework for California Public Schools, 1992 Edition (1992)	6.75
0929	Model Curriculum Standards, Grades Nine Through Twelve (1985)	5.50
0845	Physical Education Model Curriculum Standards, Grades Nine Through Twelve (1991)	5.50
0906	Quality Criteria for High Schools: Planning, Implementing, Self-Study, and Program Quality Review (1990)	5.00
0815	A Question of Thinking: A First Look at Students: Performance on Open-ended Questions in Mathematics (1989)	6.50
1038	Science Facilities Design in California Public Schools (1992)	6.25
0870	Science Framework for California Public Schools (1990)	8.00
1040	Second to None: A Vision of the New California High School (1992)	5.75
0926	Seeing Fractions: A Unit for the Upper Elementary Grades (1991)	7.50
0836	Statement on Competencies in Mathematics Expected of Entering Freshmen (1989)	5.00
0805	Visual and Performing Arts Framework for California Public Schools (1989)	7.25

* The price for 100 booklets is $30; the price for 1,000 booklets is $230. A set of one of each of the parent booklets in English is $3.

† Also available without binder for $5.75 (item no. 0801).

‡ This single copy price is available to California residents only. The residence stipulation also applies to multiple quantities: 2–9 copies, $4.25 each (item no. 9973); and 10 or more copies, $3.00 each (item no. 9972). Please state quantity.

Orders should be directed to:

California Department of Education
P.O. Box 271
Sacramento, CA 95812-0271

Please include the item number for each title ordered.

Remittance or purchase order must accompany order. Purchase orders without checks are accepted only from governmental agencies. Sales tax should be added to all orders from California purchasers. Stated prices, which include shipping charges to anywhere in the United States, are subject to change.

A complete list of publications available from the Department, including apprenticeship instructional materials, may be obtained by writing to the address listed above or by calling (916) 445-1260.

84182   R92-124 (Second printing) 003-0006-93 300 6-93 10M